HOW TO ANALYZE PEOPLE

Read Human Behaviors, Learn Body Language, And Analyze Nonverbal Communication Using Emotional Intelligence

Samantha Scott

© Copyright 2020 by Samantha Scott. All right reserved.

The work contained herein has been produced with the intent to provide relevant knowledge and information on the topic on the topic described in the title for entertainment purposes only. While the author has gone to every extent to furnish up to date and true information, no claims can be made as to its accuracy or validity as the author has made no claims to be an expert on this topic. Notwithstanding, the reader is asked to do their own research and consult any subject matter experts they deem necessary to ensure the quality and accuracy of the material presented herein.

This statement is legally binding as deemed by the Committee of Publishers Association and the American Bar Association for the territory of the United States. Other jurisdictions may apply their own legal statutes. Any reproduction, transmission or copying of this material contained in this work without the express written consent of the copyright holder shall be deemed as a copyright violation as per the current legislation in force on the date of publishing and subsequent time thereafter. All additional works derived from this material may be claimed by the holder of this copyright.

The data, depictions, events, descriptions and all other information forthwith are considered to be true, fair and accurate unless the work is expressly described as a work of fiction. Regardless of the nature of this work, the Publisher is exempt from any responsibility of actions taken by the reader in conjunction with this work. The Publisher acknowledges that the reader acts of their own accord and releases the author and Publisher of any responsibility for the observance of tips, advice, counsel, strategies and techniques that may be offered in this volume.

TABLE OF CONTENTS

Introduction 1
Chapter 1 *The Purpose Of Analyzing Others* 4
Chapter 2 *Can You Really Understand The Mind By Watching The Body?* 7
Chapter 3 *The Uses Of Analyzing Others* 11
Chapter 4 *Looking At Nonverbal Cues* 16
Chapter 5 *Understanding The Movements Of The Face* 22
Chapter 6 *Understanding The Movements Of The Body* 30
Chapter 7 *Understanding The Movements Of The Legs And Feet* 37
Chapter 8 *Proxemics* 43
Chapter 9 *Haptics* 48
Chapter 10 *Identifying Body Language Clusters* 51
Chapter 11 *Using Body Language* 60
Conclusion 66
Description 68

INTRODUCTION

Congratulations on purchasing *How to Analyze People,* and thank you for doing so.

Imagine that you have just encountered a person. You and the other person do not know each other at all. You look at him, and he looks at you, and you seem to have some sort of mutual understanding between the two of you. You walk around him, and he walks around you before you both head off. You then move on about your day without thinking anything of it.

A little bit later, you walk past another person. This person looks at you, and immediately, in your gut, you feel nervous. You can't explain it—you don't know what it is or why you feel that way, but, suddenly, you are afraid—more afraid than you thought you would be. What do you do? How do you approach the situation? You end up trying to beeline it out of the area that you are in. That night, you see something chilling on the news: That same person that you passed nervously was arrested for stealing something.

You don't know how you knew that this person was up to no good, but you did. You don't know how to explain it, but you chose to avoid him rather than heading further down that road, where you very well could have been the one robbed instead. How did you know? Intuition? Guardian angel? Sheer dumb luck?

Nope.

The answer is through body language. Unconsciously, you knew that this person posed a threat due to the body language that he put off. Even if he had approached you with a smile on his face, there is a very good chance that the rest of his body language would not jive. This is not some sort of magic or anything else—it is biology.

We are naturally equipped with a sense of being able to read the body language of others. We understand the importance of being able to read what someone else is doing, what they are thinking, how they choose to behave, and why they do what they do. We have evolved to be able to read the body language of other humans because of the value it brings. When you can look at your tribe and know what the rest of them are thinking or feeling in the state of nature, you can know that ultimately, you need to do something, or ultimately, everything is okay. By being able to look to the body language of other people, we get an instant snapshot of what is going on in their minds, similar to how dogs will read other dogs that they approach. The ability to read body language is not unique to humans—in fact, the vast majority of animals have some degree of body language. Typically, the more social the animal, the more complex the body language becomes as a result. So, what does this mean for you, then?

It means that learning to read body language is one of the best things that you can do for yourself. When you learn to read body language, you are able to begin interacting with people in far more effective manners. When you engage in that sort of body language with other people, you can find yourself becoming far better at understanding the minds of those around you. You can become more capable of understanding intentions as well as being more effective at communicating in general.

Overall, being able to read body language is one of the most important skills that you can learn during the course of your life, and the sooner that you develop it, the better. That is exactly what this book is here for—as you read through this book, you can expect to learn all about what it will take to learn to analyze other people. You will learn why we make it a point to analyze others, how important it becomes to be able to understand the mind of other people by watching the body, and how you can begin to use analyzing others to benefit yourself. From there, it will be time to look at what can be done to understand nonverbal cues and the process of reading people, and then it is time to address the various points to read. We will go over how to read the face, the body, the legs, and feet, and take a look at a few other types of body language as well, such as proxemics and haptics—the usage of distance and touch to help with communication. Then, we will take the time to go over how to use body language—both in reading common clusters of body language and in being able to use it to influence others as well.

As you read, you will learn everything that you will need to get started with reading other people. You will learn about being able to understand the intentions that people have, what they choose to do with themselves, and more, all by reading through this book. Keep in mind that sometimes, being able to read someone else may actually save someone's life. It can really change lives.

You will learn how you can start benefiting yourself and other people through being able to read body language as well. Did you know that sometimes, people do not know what they want, though their body language is screaming it, loud and clear for them? When you learn to appreciate this fact and approach the situation as being able to understand them, you can use that as well. You can help people. You can put them at ease if you need to. You can convince them that they want something when they are a bit iffy on the situation. Ultimately, the best way to ensure that you can put yourself in this position is to learn to read them in the first place, and that is where this book comes in. You will learn these skills that you ought to have. You will ensure that you are in a position that you can better help those around you, and it will be highly compelling for you and for those around you. So, are you ready to become a much better person? Are you ready to see how your own body language matters here? If so, then keep reading… This book is here to teach you to do exactly that.

There are plenty of books on this subject on the market; thanks again for choosing this one! Every effort was made to ensure it is full of as much useful information as possible; please enjoy!

CHAPTER 1
The Purpose Of Analyzing Others

When we think about communication, we almost always consider the idea of talking or writing. We think about words themselves. Communication becomes something that, without words, we do not really consider. After all, how much is really communicated by standing around without making a sound? The truth is—it is incredibly telling.

Communication comes primarily in two different forms. It can be used verbally, meaning with the use of words in various forms, or it can be nonverbal, in which case it is silent and without the need for sounds at all. Nonverbal communication is able to be discerned at a glance toward other people, and it is incredibly valuable. When you can communicate nonverbally, you can communicate in ways that do not require you to hear a single word spoken. You can look at someone and understand so much about them at just a glance.

This is so important when you consider the fact that people are largely social and are driven by their need to interact with each other. Being able to communicate directly with each other becomes one of the most important parts of remaining a society. Think about it—if you cannot communicate, how can you cooperate? If you have on the way to make it clear what you are thinking about or hearing said, how can you possibly make it a point to change up how you choose to engage? Ultimately, being able to address the situations that you are in requires communication, and sometimes, that communication needs to be quiet.

Of course, we also use the ability to analyze others for more than just communication as well. It is used to be able to identify the emotions of other people, which becomes a highly compelling ability to have. It allows you to begin to recognize whether someone else is attempting to deceive you, as well—when you can tell when someone is lying, you can protect yourself from the collateral damage that would come along with it. You can tell if someone has attracted you as well, thanks to recognizing the signs, and you will also be able to identify and understand the thoughts that someone else may have. Finally, when you consider the ability that you gain from being able to analyze the thoughts of other people, you discover that being able to read to other people, you get a package of communication that is undeniably important.

Being able to analyze others can be the difference between being scammed and being able to tell when someone is trying to take advantage of you. Being able to tell when someone else is being threatened or attempting to assert dominance over you is perfect. When you can do this, you know precisely when it is that people need to be addressed. You will be able to see how to cut out the nonsense so you can ensure that you are able to make judgments that are highly supported by information that you already have about something.

Analyzing Others for Identifying Emotions

When it comes to analyzing other people, you can gain all sorts of information that is highly beneficial. Perhaps one of the best parts, however, is being able to analyze others to identify their emotions as you go along the way. This is imperative—when you can see the emotions that other people have, you can then begin to figure out what it is that they do. When it comes to being able to identify the emotions of other people, you find yourself in a position where you can start to interact with them better.

Think about it—when you work together with other people, you have to be in communication with them somehow. It makes sense, then, that you would be able to read the emotional state of that person at any given point in time. If emotions themselves are designed to motivate us into acting in certain situations, when we have other people capable of understanding our motivations as well, we can coordinate far better. Think about it—if you look at your partner and see that he is angry, you can realize that something somewhere is a threat, whether that is your own direct actions or if it is something else. By being able to tell the difference, you should be able to figure out what it is that you can do to help. You can tell if the problem is that you have overstepped or if someone else has instead. By working to figure this out, little by little, you can start to piece together exactly how you need to interact.

Likewise, when you can see the emotional state of someone else, you can help them when they need it. You will be able to help them to work through their problems. Think about how, when you see someone that is sad, you naturally want to help, especially if you know the other person or have some vested interest in their behaviors. This is important to keep in mind—when you are able to do this, you start to empathize more because you are reading their body language.

Analyzing Others to Identify Lying

Another benefit of analyzing people is that you can tell when people are attempting to deceive you. There is very clear body language that can be looked at that determines when you are being deceived, and the sooner that you learn to read it, the better. Think about it—how often do you simply take people at face value when they tell you something? When you work in sensitive fields that involve important sensitive information, such as requiring social security numbers, money, and the like, you will need to ensure that you can tell if they are lying. Think about it—if you are going to sell something to someone and your business requires you to be able to make money through these sales, you want to make sure that you have a client that is not going to be problematic. If you want to ensure that you can better engage with the entire situation, you must ensure that you choose to approach the situation accordingly. This means that you need to be able to tell when someone is deceptive.

Other fields are even more sensitive—if you are a lawyer or an investigator, you will need to be able to tell when someone else is lying. You must make sure that you can see it in the face of the other person so you can ensure that you are getting the whole truth. Think about it—if you are a bankruptcy attorney and you are getting information from your client, you will be submitting that information to the court of law, and you must be as honest as possible, or you risk perjury charges. This means that you need to be disclosing all information as required by law. If your client lies to you, you need to be able to spot it.

This is also important in interpersonal relationships as well—you must be able to tell what is going on with those around you. If you are being asked to help someone or loan something to a friend, you want to know that they are willing to pay it back as agreed. You must be able to see that your friends are honest and truthful and that they are not trying to take you for a ride at your expense. Being able to read when someone is deceiving you has so many benefits in just about every single aspect of your life, and it all begins with being able to see the truth in the matter. It all starts with analyzing people and their body language to get the fullest picture of the situation.

Analyzing Others to Identify Attraction

Analyzing others also matters in the dating scene, believe it or not. When you know what to look for in terms of body language, you can start to spot the people that are attracted or interested in you. Think about it—if you are heading out into the dating scene, you want to know where you have a chance and where you may not. You will be able to see when someone appears to be attracted to you so you can identify whether you have a chance. You will also be able to use this as a sort of metric for whether your date is actually interested in you in the first place.

Would you really want to waste your time on a date with someone that is not interested in you? Would you really want to spend time trying to force a date with someone that does not seem driven to continue? Most people would not—and because of that, you want to be able to tell what is going on with other people in their minds to control how you engage with everyone around you. Ultimately, the more that you go through the effort of doing so, the more that you will realize that being able to read the other person.

CHAPTER 2
Can You Really Understand The Mind By Watching The Body?

Now, you might be doubtful that you can actually understand the mind and what is going on inside of it just by looking at the body, but the truth is, you can tell an awful lot just by taking a look at what other people are doing. This is why you get that gut reaction when someone charges at you to tell their intent. You can tell the difference between whether someone runs toward you happily or angrily all by looking at the body language. This is more than just facial features, too—it is all about everything. Body language is visible in how people move, how they position themselves, what they do with touching other people, how they relate to each other, and more. When it comes to being able to tell how people engage, you can tell so much through paying attention to those little movements and actions.

As you read through this book, you will be guided through understanding this nonverbal communication so you can better read it. You will be able to tell what it is that someone is thinking for one simple reason: The body will almost always betray the mind. Your unconscious thoughts that drive everything are highly visible just by learning to analyze the body itself. Think about it—you can tell from a glance when someone is shy versus when they are simply uninterested in being around other people.

Before we start delving into how to analyze people, let's take a look at the science behind it. Within this chapter, we are going to address the idea of body language as an unconscious manifestation of the thoughts that you have within your own mind. With that approach, you can begin to see what it will take to understand the minds of those around you. You will discover how you can better understand and interpret the thoughts just by virtue of being able to do some backward sleuthing. Through backtracking through the thoughts, you can then begin to recognize what is going on inside the minds of those around you. When you are able to piece together that backtrack, you get to see precisely what is happening inside the minds of the other people. As you learn to understand their minds, you get to also influence them as well. Through being able to influence them as well, you will be able to figure out what you must do with them. You will be able to find ways that you can better assume how you will engage with the other person to grant yourself that added level of control that you were looking for.

The Body Betrays the Mind
When it comes to being able to read the mind, your body will always betray your mind. This is because your body language is primarily controlled by your subconscious mind. The subconscious mind is

responsible for your ability to respond and react to the world around you—it is there to help you understand how to engage with the world around you. When you are going about your day, your mind is primarily focused entirely on what you are doing at any given moment. Think about it—you are probably currently focused on how you are reading this book right now. You are not paying attention to the surroundings, at least not consciously. You are not actively listening to other people or what they are talking about. You are not paying attention to the television show that is on in front of you. You are not doing anything but read these words across the page. However, if you were to hear something that was pertinent to you, such as someone saying your name, you would hear it. This is because your unconscious mind is listening to everything in the background. Though you may not be paying attention yourself, your unconscious mind is listening to everything that is going on around you. It is filtering out anything that you need to pay attention to while ignoring everything else. As a result, you will find that ultimately, you can do better—you can respond well to the surroundings because you paid just enough attention.

Your subconscious mind is important when it comes to how you navigate through the world. Think about it—when you go through life with your unconscious mind as your copilot, you are constantly absorbing information from all around you, even if you are not really paying attention to it. This is why something moving in the corner of your eye can catch your attention, or hearing someone call your name will snap you out of whatever you are doing. Your subconscious mind is paying attention, and it will then respond by pushing that particular stimulus to your conscious mind.

This is imperative to understand—when you recognize this, you will see that ultimately, you can better understand the next concept that we are about to discuss, and that is that the subconscious mind is also directly responsible for controlling your body language as well. Your subconscious cannot directly communicate with your conscious mind—but, it can influence how you feel. It can also influence how it reads the body language of other people. As a result, the way that you approach most situations is highly dependent upon your subconscious mind.

Imagine this situation for a moment—you are taking a walk around the park. You don't know anyone that is present there as you are not in your usual neighborhood. You walk along, and suddenly, you feel a sensation of nervousness. You cannot explain it—but you feel concerned about something. As you walk around, you cannot figure out what it is that is bothering you, but it is clear that there is something. You walk around, you think about it, and you cannot identify those feelings of doubt. However, the more that you walk, the more that you feel that way. Eventually, you realize what it is-- it is the fact that there is someone that has been near you at every turn through the park. Something about his body language is setting off that instinct within yourself that you must be cautious around him. You can't explain it, but the feeling is there. As a result, you find yourself paying more attention to him, and he leaves.

Your subconscious is what caught on to the fact that you needed to be more cautious. It warned you that you needed to pay attention at that moment so you would be safe, and it let you know that ultimately, you needed to pay attention. Likewise, it changed your own body language as well.

The Cycle of Thoughts, Feelings, and Behaviors

This happens because human behavior exists within a cycle. Your thoughts influence your feelings, which influence your behaviors. This is quite simple to understand and is something that is highly recognized throughout psychology in general. Your thoughts are directly related to how you interpret the world around you. Largely, they are based on those subconscious judgments that you make as you navigate through the world. The more that you experience something without challenging it, the more that your subconscious mind comes to accept it. Your subconscious recognizes that your lack of correction is an effective agreement and, therefore, will react accordingly.

Your thoughts are powerful. They create the emotions that you feel. Have you ever been sitting somewhere and realized that you were frustrated or angry about something? You might not know why you are so angry at the moment, but you know that you are, and as a result, you have to stop and think closer about it. What is it that is pushing you to feel that way? You think about it and realize that ultimately, it is often due to something entirely unrelated to everything else that you are doing. This is imperative to remember—often, it is an entirely unrelated thought that was the problem all along that created so many issues for you. If you keep this in mind, you can start to see what it is that happens inside the mind of someone else.

Your emotions have a very important role—they serve to keep you motivated to respond to the situation that you are in. Each emotion will have its own evolutionary purpose that is related to keeping you alive. They all work together to provide those instinctive actions that you follow when you allow your emotions to rule you. This is important to keep in mind—it means that if you feel yourself feeling emotional and then motivated toward a specific action, it is probably for a reason. The emotions that you feel can be broken down into just seven:

- **Happiness:** You feel happy to motivate yourself to repeat that behavior again. It is something that was rewarding for some reason, and you instinctively want to reinforce it.
- **Sadness:** You feel sadness when you have done something that caused a loss of some sort. Usually, this is something such as someone got hurt or was lost. You feel sadness to remind yourself

that repeating that action would be problematic for several different reasons. It motivates you to seek comfort and help from others.
- **Anger:** Anger motivates you to fight back. Usually, it is the result of feeling threatened for some reason or another and is designed to cause you to protect yourself or those around you.
- **Fear:** Fear is your motivation to protect yourself from a threat that you cannot fight off. When you feel fear, you feel a need to escape at all costs. Fear may become angry if you have a way to conceivably fight your way out of the problem. It will usually lead to you attempting to find an out from a situation, or lashing out.
- **Surprise:** Surprise is your body's reaction to needing to pay more attention to whatever it is that is happening around you. It drives you to focus on whatever is in front of you so you can address the situation.
- **Contempt:** Contempt is the feeling that is meant to motivate you to avoid someone. It is effectively disgust and anger combined and directed to one person.
- **Disgust**: Disgust is meant to make you avoid something that is no good for you. You feel disgusted when you are exposed to something that is rotten, either literally or figuratively. It is meant to keep you away from the situation and far from getting involved with it. When you feel disgusted, you tell yourself that you must avoid whatever it is.

As you can see, your emotions have a very important purpose, and you owe it to yourself to understand them. These emotions become highly motivating and create behaviors if you are not attempting to consciously outweigh them. Yes, you can make it a point to change up your behaviors yourself, but it is not always that easy. If you don't know what you are doing, you can end up stuck. You can find yourself controlled by your emotions. However, this means that you can also typically look at what other people are doing to understand them as well. If you wanted to understand what is going on in someone else's mind, you would look at their behaviors because the behaviors will follow.

Think of it this way—if you see someone running toward you with a scowl and overall very threatening body language, you can assume that they are furious about something. Through understanding that they are furious, you can then look around and figure out what the problem is. Did you just cut him off in the parking lot? He might be annoyed that you snatched up a spot. Did you offend him somehow? If so, figure it out.

By being able to follow these patterns in this manner, you can help yourself to figure out what to do next. You can look at people and understand the mindsets that they are taking through everything that they do.

CHAPTER 3
The Uses Of Analyzing Others

When it comes to being able to analyze others, you have several key benefits that can help you, and there are several situations that you can use your analysis of others to help yourself as well. When you learn what it will take to analyze other people, you can then begin to utilize it as much as possible. The more that you utilize it, the more likely that you are to find a way that you can better the situation entirely. Think about it this way—you can stop and consider the fact that you are looking at the actions to read the minds of those around you. This is something that we have already made quite clear. Now, all you will need to do is make sure that you are taking the time to recognize the ways that this can benefit you.

In this chapter, we will address several key ways that you can utilize the ability to analyze others to help yourself in real-life scenarios. We will see several key uses that can benefit just about anyone. Whether you are introverted, extroverted, interested in other people, or not, being able to read people is a skill that everyone should have.

Better Negotiating

When you start to negotiate with people, you are setting out to come up with some sort of agreement between parties. You and someone else will be sitting down and walking through all of the steps of figuring out what it is that you want and where that common ground between you lies. It could be that you want one thing, and they want another, and you need to figure out which concessions that you are willing to make. However, it is difficult for you to ensure that your negotiations are on the right foot when you and the other person are not really willing to work with each other. This prevents you from being able to work well with everyone involved. However, what you can do is learn how you can better engage through being able to read body language.

Imagine this: You are sitting in front of the other person, and they do not appear to be very open to being negotiated with in the first place. Do you think that you are going to get very far? Perhaps they are sitting there, arms crossed, and looking away from you because they do not really want to engage. The chances are, they do not want to be involved with you at all- they do not want to have to deal with you, so they try to avoid doing so. They shut down their body language.

When you can see this in someone else, you can tell that they are not currently open to that negotiation in the first place. This means that what you can do is take the time that you will need to stop and think. You will be able to tell yourself that you do not want to deal with the situation, and you will not be as effective as if they were more open. You know this—and yet you are stuck. In this instance, the best thing that you can do is ensure that you are going to find a way to better engage. When you can find that best set of engagement, you can then begin to figure out what it will take to better encourage the other person to open up.

Through being able to read the other person, you can then begin to figure out how best to engage. You will figure out what it will take for you to actually talk to them. You will learn how you can actually properly interact with them. This is imperative—you will be able to ensure that ultimately, you are happier with the situation at hand. This matters immensely—you must make sure that you are in a position in which you can better engage. When you get to that point, you know that you will be able to negotiate more effectively. You have to learn how to open up their body language by using your own to influence them. Over time, you then get them to be more willing to engage with you, and as a result, you get to negotiate.

Better Selling

Similarly, you can use your ability to read people's body language to land sales. This is especially true if you find yourself working with someone that may not actually be as well informed about their own body language. If you find that you are looking at someone that appears to not be very familiar with their own body language, you can realize that you can actually tell more about their mindset than they can. This can be useful, for example, if you are attempting to convince them to buy something. By being able to tell what they think when they struggle with it themselves, you are able to start pinpointing what it is that they want.

Being able to read their body language also lets you know if you are on the right track to getting what they want right. Think about it—if you are selling a car, you would want to make sure that you are getting the right taste down for what they want. This means that you would want to make sure that you are paying attention to the reactions that they have as you are going through everything. You can tell by watching their body language closely whether they are actually interested in what you are showing them or if you are actually on the wrong track, and they are just trying to be polite. By being able to figure this out little by little, you can help yourself to figure out precisely what it is that you should be offering them.

Consider, for example, showing them a red minivan. You can tell by their reaction if they are enthusiastic about it, whether they need convincing, or if you are entirely on the wrong track. Being able to watch their reaction tells you whether you should redirect them to something else or if what is going to be best in this situation is going toward something else entirely. The more that you do this and the more you get used to reading the other person, the more likely that you are to actually successfully convince them of whatever it is that you are trying to convince them to buy.

This can be used in any sort of sales-based job. When you can tell what it is that will drive someone to purchase; you can take advantage of the situation. You will be able to get those sales just because you will know what it is that someone wants. Take, for example, the idea that people tend to orient themselves, so their feet point at what it is that they want at the moment. Most people do not realize this, and it is so unconscious anyway that they do not quite catch on to what they are doing. However, once you know this, you can look at the direction of the feet when you are regarding a customer. If you can see that their feet are pointing toward the exit, you can assume they want to go, whereas if you see their feet pointing in the direction of a certain item, you can presume that they want to approach it.

Better Interviewing Skills

When it comes to looking at interviewing skills, being able to read people is, once again, something that can be incredibly useful, whether you are the interviewer or the interviewee. When you are the one doing the interviewing, being able to read what the other person is thinking or feeling becomes highly important—it helps you to ensure that you are on the right track with the other person. It ensures that you are able to read just how confident or honest the other person is being. When it comes to seeing that confidence or honesty, you can tell a lot about someone. Imagine that you have just asked them to answer a question about a time that they were able to overcome a problem—if you know what you are looking for, you can identify when they are lying about if they are. You will also be able to tell if they are telling the truth. This means that you can be an incredibly intuitive interviewer that will help you to show yourself whether or not you are actually paying close attention to the situation. When you are able to tell what is going on with those that you interview, you can truly choose the strongest of the candidates because you can better and more comfortably read them.

Additionally, as someone that is on the other side of the situation, if you are the one being interviewed, you can tell just how well the interview is going by virtue of understanding the body language that goes into the situation as well. Being able to tell what they are thinking and feeling at any point in time is highly powerful. It will help you immensely to ensure that you can better cope with the situation that you are involved in. You can tell if you are losing interest form the interviewer or if the interviewer does not seem to like you much. The more that you are able to tell just how liked or disliked you are, the more likely you are to be able to get through the interview well. Think about it—you can use that reading of the other person's body language to help yourself to figure out precisely what it is that you will need to better the situation that you are in. When you learn how to identify what you are doing and how you are doing it, you realize that ultimately, you can tweak your body language to make yourself that much more attractive of an interviewer.

Being able to read each other in these situations where you are closely intertwined with each other becomes imperative—being able to show yourself that you do know what to expect and how to read the other people will set you up for success. This is crucial—if you want to thrive, then you want to ensure that you are putting yourself in a situation where you can do so.

Better Leadership Skills

people, you must make sure that you are paying close attention to the situation at hand. Finally, consider the boost to leadership skills when you know how to read people as well. If you have ever read a book on emotional intelligence, you would know that one of the most defining features of a good leader is someone that is able to understand and motivate the people that they are trying to lead. When you can read what someone else is thinking or feeling, you can ensure that everyone is on the same page, while also being able to defuse conflicts before they have a chance to get bad enough to cause problems. The more that you work with yourself, the more that you can realize that ultimately, you will be in a position where you can better engage. Think about it: If you are going to be trying to lead people, you need to ensure that you are in a position where you feel like you can tell what it is that the people around you are thinking or feeling. When it turns out that what they are feeling or thinking is positive, they will usually be more inclined to help or follow through with what you need.

Good leaders are those who are able to ensure that they are pushing people in the right direction for the right reason. When you are able to figure out what it is that drives them, you are able to see that they want to follow you. You will be able to make them feel confident in you, and that is how you know that you are effective. Ultimately, the best leaders will be able to read their followers and will take great pleasure in figuring out what they can do and how they can engage with everyone else.

Learning to read people can help when you are giving a speech to people; for example—you will be able to tell if people understand what you are saying or if you need to start changing up the level of difficulty that you will speak. It will help you to tell if people agree with what you are saying or if you are causing problems with the way that you are approaching a situation. Being able to tell what everyone else wants and thinks means that you will be able to better motivate people for this reason.

One on one, you can show that you are a good listener when you are analyzing body language—you will pick up on those nonverbal cues as well that will help you to figure out what it will take for you to better get along with those around you. When you can better relate to everyone involved, you will show yourself that you can better speak to them. You will be able to show yourself that you are someone that is more capable of navigating through these situations. You will show yourself precisely what you must do if you want to be able to engage well with those around you.

Ultimately, being able to read other people becomes something that is highly beneficial to you. If you want to be able to understand what is going on in the minds of others, you must learn to read their body language so you can begin to understand them as individuals as well as better. The more that you can do this, the better that you will do in engaging with those around you.

Analyzing other people, then, becomes one of your most crucial tools when it comes to being able to better yourself and your interactions with people. If you want to do well, you must make sure that you are taking the time to better the situation to the best of your ability. The more that you do this, the better the situation will be.

CHAPTER 4
Looking At Nonverbal Cues

Understanding what other people are thinking or feeling starts with looking at the nonverbal. It starts by looking at how people behave and what their bodies are saying without listening to the words. Nonverbal communication might be more primitive than directly stating what you are thinking or feeling, but that doesn't make it any less effective—after all, nature has used nonverbal cues for millennia in animals. The entirety of social animals communicate nonverbally—they have all sorts of different ways that they are able to get their points across. Even bees have a complex form of communication through their movements that allow other bees to know where they need to go.

Nonverbal communication makes up the bulk of any communication that you will do, and that is what makes it so important to use and understand. It is something that you must learn to understand so you *can* see what is going on behind the scenes. For this reason, we will dedicate this chapter to going over what nonverbal communication is, what to look at when trying to understand it, and how to read it. When it comes to being able to read other people, you are looking for how they move.

Defining Nonverbal Communication

Defining nonverbal communication is simple: It is communication that your body does nonverbally. This means that it happens without words. However, there is more to it than just that—nonverbal communication is unconscious. When you communicate nonverbally, your body will create cues that are sent to those around you. People around you then are able to receive those signals that you send out and translate and understand them.

Your communication with other people does consist of the words that you say, but there is more to it as well. The minuscule movements that you make are interpreted by the people around you without them being aware of it. That's what causes people to get those gut feelings about others when they were talking. If you've ever had that feeling when talking to someone that they were lying, you've had it before. You know that feeling—that sensation that you are in a position in which someone is going to be dangerous, or when someone is problematic in other ways. Likewise, you can see when they're more amicable as well. Being able to understand that nonverbal communication is critical, and your mind reads it without thinking about it. You can tell when someone is threatening no matter where they are from. You can tell when someone is happy to see you, regardless of their culture or place of origin. This is because we can all read very similar body language. We know that certain movements are aggressive, even innately. Your body knows this, as makes your mind and your unconscious mind makes it a point to go through everything.

Of course, it is important to note that nonverbal language can also take the place of sounds that are made. Groaning or sighing, for example, involves making sounds, but there are no words that are formed. It is nonverbal for that reason alone. Verbal communication involves the utilization of words in several forms, from being able to write something down to speaking it out loud. Nonverbal communication, then, is anything else. If it is not filled up with words, it is nonverbal communication. When you start to recognize nonverbal communication as actually making up the bulk of everything that we convey to each other, you start recognizing just how powerful it is.

What to Look at for Nonverbal Language

When it comes to being able to read nonverbal communication, there are a few easy places that you can look—when you are reading it in other people, there are a handful of things to consider. Each of the different kinds of nonverbal communication becomes imperative for you to be able to discuss. These different forms of nonverbal communication that you ought to pay attention to are kinesics, oculesics, haptics, proxemics, and vocalics.

Kinesics

Kinesics refers to the general body language that you display at any point in time. It is the movements, the general expressions, and the demeanor that your body takes on. This is kinesthetic—referring to movement. When you keep this in mind, you can keep track of what it is with ease. The bulk of what you will be learning to read in this book is kinesic in nature just due to the fact that there are so many more kinesic factors that come into play when it comes to looking at nonverbal body language.

Oculesics

Oculesics refers to the movements of the eyes. While it is technically indicative of a form of kinesics, it is also quite focused, and for that reason, it gets its own special consideration. It is the ability to understand the movements of eyes in general, from how they open, close, gaze at things, and more. This is imperative to understand so you can be certain that you can read the windows to the soul, as they are commonly referred to.

Haptics

Haptics allows you to utilize touch to communicate. Different touches can convey widely different concepts, especially when you consider the ways that touch can vary so dramatically. Touch can go from something that you use to gently encourage someone to push them away or lashing out at them. Even a brief touch can be enough to communicate something important, and that must be considered heavily.

Proxemics

Proxemics refers to the utilization of space in order to communicate topics or concepts. It can be both vertical and horizontal, referring to how you position yourself above or around someone else. When you look at proxemics, you are looking at how a boss may attempt to tower over a person that is being scolded, or how someone who is uninterested in someone else will stand further away from them.

Vocalics

Finally, vocalics refers to the way in which you use your voice to communicate nonverbally. It consists of how you talk to others, what you do with them around, or how you make sounds. Laughing, groaning, sighing, screeching, humming, and other such sounds are all examples of nonverbal communication that you can use with others, and they all involve you being able to communicate something.

All of these come together to create the nonverbal communication that you use—they are important to consider. They all matter to ensure that you can better understand and even influence other people, and we will be working on learning to read this. Nonverbal communication is an integral part of being able to communicate in general, and without it, you cannot hope to understand the full picture that you hear when you are interacting. You will not see everything for what things are when you cannot communicate or see what the undertones are. You must be able to read those undertones so you can be certain that you do understand what is going on.

Learning to Read People

Reading other people is something that you will need to learn to be successful in many different situations, and thankfully, it doesn't have to be hard. With just a few steps, you can begin to understand what is going on in other people's minds so you can then begin to interpret their actions and feelings. Your own actions and feelings will be influenced by other people—and because of that, being able to read theirs as well becomes imperative. Thankfully, you can follow this guide:

Step 1: Identify personality type

To begin understanding the people around you, you must start with determining the personality type of the other person. There are all sorts of ways that you can do this, but the easiest is to identify a few simple factors that come into play as you watch someone. You will be watching how they navigate as well as how they respond. In looking at this, you will start to understand the kind of person that you are exposed to.

First, consider the difference between sensing or being intuitive. This is the first difference that you will be looking at. Some people tend to orient themselves with the use of their senses—they look for support and facts that help others end up being more intuitive in nature- they focus on what it is that they are feeling at any point in time. This is imperative to pay attention to. When you watch the personality type and pay attention to how someone chooses to navigate in the world, you start to see new patterns. You see into their minds and how they think—this is imperative to recognize their behaviors. This beginning point will provide that insight for you.

Then, you must consider whether they react to the world through thoughts or feelings. Are they focusing on making sure that they satisfy their emotions? Are they looking for ways for them to feel content? Are they looking for ways to think about their situations? Thinking individuals tend to be more driven by their own rationality and logic than anything else—they will intentionally respond to the world through following preset and predetermined rules. They are more likely to abide by those rules. Feeling individuals, on the other hand, are driven by their emotions. They consider values and the situation at hand rather than trying to force it into a situation that I can naturally fall into.

When you start to consider this, you can then address whether the person that you are speaking to is introverted or extroverted. The introverts are those that seem to orient themselves within themselves—they are quieter because they are caught up in their own thoughts and feelings at the time. They focus on themselves and how they behave, and they often find themselves drained being around other people too much. They are more likely to be quietly observing when they are in a group, and they look like they may be overwhelmed when they are pushed into the limelight.

Extroverts, on the other hand, tend to love being the center of attention. They love to be around other people to interact—they feel the best when they are able to engage well with others. They act rather than think, and they are usually much more at ease in social settings.

Step 2: Get the base reading of their body language

Then, when you have that base reading of what kind of person you are trying to read, you can start focusing on getting a base reading. It is important to know what is going on in their mind before getting started so you can tell whether what is happening appears to be characteristic or not. Think about it—an introvert probably would not be running around with their hands up in the air for no reason, and an extrovert probably would not be averting their gaze in a conversation. Understanding this will help you to begin to read the base body language to figure out just how natural it is.

Getting the base reading of someone else's body language becomes incredibly important before you start reading. This will give you a general guideline to understanding what is going on inside the mind of the other person. Think about it—if you are driving your car and realize that you are getting 20 miles to the gallon, how would you feel about it? Would you think that is a good thing or a bad thing? The answer is entirely dependent upon the base MPG that you expect. A truck getting 20 miles to the gallon may actually be somewhat decent—many of them are notorious gas guzzlers. A brand new Prius only getting 20 miles to the gallon, on the other hand, is indicative that something is catastrophically wrong—the MPG is almost halved. This consideration is important: You must be able to understand what is going on, but you also have to have that context as well. You must be able to tell whether what is happening is actually a good or a bad thing by comparing it to the natural state.

In terms of body language, that means taking a look at natural states. If you want to read someone well as you engage, you must see their default body language before you begin. This is most often done either by watching the other person interact without any pressure or by having a general basic conversation with someone else if you are getting ready to try to read them. During that general basic conversation, make it a point to pay close attention to how they engage with you. How are they holding themselves? What are they doing with themselves? Pay attention to their demeanor and figure out how they are more likely to stand.

Step 3: Look for discrepancies in their body language

Next, consider looking for any discrepancies. This happens during the interaction now- when you go through the motions and start looking at how you engage with each other, you start to see where those discrepancies begin and what they mean. Looking at those means that you will be able to see the different behaviors. This is where their body language will begin to tell you everything that you need to know. You will be able to see how the person is engaging with you during your interaction. Are they uncharacteristically being shy? Are they averting their eyes a lot? Are they batting their eyes at you? Start looking for the signs. Start looking around at how they behave. Note anything that does not match up with the original baseline body language that you identified and make sure that you take the time and effort to pay closer attention to it.

Step 4: Identify the clusters of behaviors

Next, you must start building up clusters of behaviors. This is where you start to consider the context of the body language that you see. Are they averting their eyes because they are scared or because they are lying to you? You may need to look at other body languages to see exactly what is going on with them. By beginning to understand those different clusters of behavior, you can then begin to understand what you are doing and how you are doing it. You will be able to understand how everything plays out together.

For example, imagine a woman who is looking down at the floor. She could be nervous, shy, or also just uncomfortable. She could be embarrassed as well. What you need to pay attention to, then, is everything else alongside it. You need to look for the other signs to tell the difference. Someone who is nervous may also cross their arms and shift in hopes of being able to self-soothe, or someone who is embarrassed may also be blushing uncontrollably and stuttering. You need to look at other signs to see what is going on.

When it comes to identifying clusters of behaviors, you will want to pay attention to whether you see the same behaviors play out over and over again. You are looking for signs that the behaviors are repeating over and over again, that they are not just one-off coincidences. Being sure that you are considerate of this point will help you to ensure that you can get the cleanest reading possible.

Step 5: Interpreting the clusters of behaviors

Finally, the last step in all of this is making sure that you analyze it. Look at the behaviors, the feelings, and then start to figure out why they are what they are. Pay attention to the way that people tend to engage. Consider the situation that they are in. Does their reaction make sense? Do they seem like they are out of proportion? All of these factors will help you to figure out what you should be doing and how you should be taking the behaviors that you are exposed to. The sooner that you learn how to read those behaviors, the sooner you can start to interpret them.

CHAPTER 5
Understanding The Movements Of The Face

For the most part, when people think about reading others, they look to the face. They think that if they are going to be reading anything about the other person, it will happen by looking at the expressions that they make. This is true to some degree—the face will almost always be the first place people look just instinctively. If you are talking to someone, you naturally look at their face when you are trying to figure out their thoughts that they have. When you do this, you are checking out several different aspects—you are looking at them in the eye, which acknowledges they are there. However, you will also be looking at them in several other ways as well. You will see their eyebrows and mouth as well while looking at their general expression in hopes of getting more information about them.

Ultimately, the face is one of the easiest places to start—but it is also the one place that people will tend to control when they want to hide their emotions. If you see that someone is trying to lie, they will almost always betray themselves in the face—they will know to try to alter their facial expressions in an attempt to lie to you. While this is a great starting point, you will need to remember that it must be taken in tandem with all other aspects of facial features and expressions, as we will explain throughout the book.

Within this chapter, we have a few key objectives: We will be identifying the universal expressions that you can expect to see no matter the person. We will then go body part by body part on the face to start looking at common body language. In particular, we will be discussing the eyes, the eyebrows, the forehead, the cheeks, the lips, and the mouth.

Universal Expressions

Did you know that there are several expressions that humans make that are universal? There are seven of them that are common across all cultures. They are commonly referred to as universal expressions, and they help to support the idea that there are certain emotions that are largely universal as well regardless of culture. These universal expressions are precisely what they may sound like—they will be identified by anyone around the world no matter where they come from, and they can actually be found in blind individuals that have never actually seen another person's face before.

If this sounds impossible, think about dogs. If you take a newborn puppy from its mother and raise it, there are certain aspects of its body language that are universal—they will happen whether they know the meaning of the wag or not. We, like dogs, have our own set of universal body language. After all, if you take a dog from the US and drop it off in Japan, it will still be able to communicate with the other dogs through body language. Likewise, your expressions will be recognized no matter where in the world that you go.

Happiness
The emotion of happiness is felt when you have met your needs or done something that is satisfying or pleasant. Generally speaking, happiness is expressed through relaxed and sometimes even excited body language. There may be a smile that bares teeth, or the mouth may be closed with lips turned upward. Either way, however, you are looking out for the Duchenne smile—the real smile where the corners of the eyes begin to crinkle. This is how you know that happiness is legitimate and not meant to just throw you off. Additionally, you may see that the eyebrows are pulled up as well.

Sadness
Sadness is perhaps the hardest of the emotions to fake—it is something that has very distinctive features. In particular, you can expect to see that the eyebrows will lower with the inner corners raising upward and pulling together. This causes a wrinkling effect between and above the brows. Additionally, you will see that the jaw pulls upwards while the bottom lip pouts outward at the same time.

Anger
Anger is going to involve the entire face. When you face an angry person, you will see them lower their eyebrows together while also pulling them inward to furrow into a V shape. The eyelids will usually tense up around the eyes, which stare harshly. Additionally, you can expect to see the lips being forced together into a thin line, or they may be open with the mouth in a square shape. The jaw, when closed, maybe either tense or jutting out.

Fear
Fear is identifiable by the eyebrows as they pull up and together at the center of the forehead. This creates a worrying furrow, and the brows themselves flatten instead of arching out. As this happens, you will note that the eyelid above the eyes is what rises upward to allow for access to seeing the whites above the iris rather than below. At the same time, the mouth is typically open with lips that pull back.

Surprise
Surprise can sometimes be mistaken for fear, largely because of the fact that you can see the whites of the eyes with both. However, with surprise, you should expect to see the whites all around the iris instead of just above. Additionally, you will expect to see some wrinkling along the forehead with an open, slack jaw lacking tension. The brows will arch and curve as they raise up, and usually, the skin between the brow and the eye is stretched taut.

Contempt
When you see contempt in someone else, you usually notice it because they raise up just one side of the mouth and eyebrow. It is a quick flash of a sneer, usually only lasting a second or two before it disappears.

Disgust
Disgust has a very important design for the expression that can help you to remember it. In disgust, you can expect to see the face all coming inward to protect your eyes, nose, and mouth, all of which are quite sensitive and require protection to ensure that they do not get damaged from toxins of any kind. The eyebrows lower to shield your eyes while your lips pull upward while your nose wrinkles in an attempt to protect the nose. The cheeks will also squeeze upward to help shield the eyes.

Reading the Eyes
Eyes are commonly called the windows to your soul for a reason—they are incredibly expressive. When you glance at someone else's eyes, you do a few important things. One, you acknowledge that they are there and present. This is majorly important—when you do this, you show them that you are actively paying attention to them. You show that you are actively watching to show that you are giving them your attention. Being able to pay attention to the eyes usually comes with its own benefits by taking the time to read the gaze, pupil dilation, and the amount of eye contact that is made.

Reading Gaze
The gaze will tell you an awful lot about the person that you are looking at. In particular, there are two key aspects that you will want to consider when attempting to read the gaze of someone else. You must look at the location and the duration. However, when you learn to understand how to read this part of the body, you can get a clear idea of what is going on in someone else's mind.

- **Location of the gaze:** if you see that someone is looking at something, there is a good chance that they want it. A glance at the door says that someone is done talking while staring down a piece of cake can imply that the cake is the object of desire at that moment. When you learn to follow someone else's gaze, you can usually figure out what it is that has drawn attraction and then figure out whether the attention is good or bad by looking at the rest of the body language
- **Duration of the gaze:** The amount of time spent staring at something is also indicative of important points as well. When you look at the duration of someone else's gaze toward something else, you start to figure out what it will take to understand what they are doing and thinking. You want to ensure that you know that they are directly driven by whatever it is that they are looking

at. Typically, the longer that someone stares at something, the more important it is to them or the more interesting that they find it.

Reading eye contact
When you want to read eye contact with someone else, you want to keep in mind that generally speaking, eye contact is something that can be quite intense. It can be very rapidly construed as wrong or too forceful and direct if you do not know what you are doing. However, not enough eye contact is also deemed problematic as it implies that you are not actually interested or that you are lying about something. Just the right amount of eye contact is having eye contact, roughly 70% of the time. Keep in mind that if you stare too much, you will be deemed aggressive, and that will give you the exact opposite of what you are trying to achieve.

Reading pupil dilation
Pupil dilation occurs when the pupils of the eyes start to expand. However, it is also quite difficult to notice if you are not right next to someone else or if you find that they have an eye color that is darker and will help to obscure the pupil. However, if you look at the eyes closed, you may be able to identify when the pupils are dilated. The thing about pupil dilation is that it is impossible to falsify—there is no way for you to consciously control the dilation of your pupils, and as such, it is something that is fairly reliable to use.

Typically, pupils will dilate when you look at someone or something that you want or are attracted to. When you find something more attractive, you will usually have more dilation of the pupil. It is also the case, however, that the pupils will dilate in response to mental processing as well. If you are trying to do complex math, for example, the pupils will dilate as a result.

Reading the Eyebrows
The eyebrows have a lot to say about the people that they belong to. They sort of frame the eyes and create an additional degree of expression. When you take a look at the eyebrows, you see that arch over the eyes that are free to move in most directions. In particular, you will find that looking at the eyebrows will tell you a lot. Take a look at the following signs.

Raised
Raising the brows tends to imply that you want to absorb more of your surroundings. You may be raising them to see more or to also emphasize something that you want to ask as well. It could, for example, create a need to convey a question or to show doubt over a situation as well.

Raising inner corners
By raising the inner corners of your eyebrows, especially when you pull them together in the center, you show either anxiety or relief. You will have to look at other signs to determine which is more appropriate in this instance.

Lowered
When you lower your eyebrows, you are hooding your eyes, as if you are hiding them from view. You are also showing that your line of sight has honed in on one thing, in particular, implying that you are highly focused on whatever it is that you are staring at. This is typically indicative of annoyance or dominance, though it can also show anger depending upon the other signs of the face as well.

Lowering center
When it comes to taking a look at the center of the brows, they can sometimes furrow together to make a V shape. When this happens, there are slight wrinkles there that create the shape in the first place. Usually, this is a sign of concentration or potential frustration.

Lowering and raising repeatedly
When the brows come up and down repeatedly, especially rapidly, you are wiggling them. This typically either wants to get attention from someone else or even acknowledge that they are present. You can also use it to show an exaggerated shock.

Reading the Cheeks
Cheeks make up the bulk of your face, and yet they are often forgotten when it comes time to read body language. However, they are quite important to pay attention to, and you will want to focus on them to the best of your ability. Ultimately, looking at the cheeks will help you to figure out what you are doing when also considering other body parts at the same time. When you learn to read the cheeks, you will get an extra glimpse into the mindset of the other person.

Cheeks pulled in
When cheeks are pulled in, you can usually assume that the other person is feeling annoyed, especially if you can also see signs of the lips being pursed as well. This is highly important to consider, as well. You usually want to avoid bothering someone if they are like this.

Cheeks blown out
If you see that their cheeks are blown outward, you see them expanding them out. They are puffed, and this typically happens out of sheer exaggeration as a sign of being unsure what to do next or feeling like you are somewhat overwhelmed with everything that you have to get done. When you consider this action, you usually are showing signs of great disapproval.

Cheeks turning red
When cheeks begin to turn red, it is usually out of embarrassment or anger over a situation. Look for other cues that can help you to clarify what they seem to be thinking.

Cheeks paling
When cheeks start to turn pale on the other hand, you can see that the blood has rushed out of their faces. This usually shows that the blood has redirected elsewhere, such as into the legs to run. It is often a sign of fear or uncertainty. However, it could also be a sign that it is simply cold outside.

Chewing on the inside of the cheek
When you chew on the inside of your cheek, you imply that you are nervous about the current situation for some reason. You show that you are a bit uncertain about how everything is going, and it is a form of trying to self-soothe. It can also be a sign of trying to avoid speaking words that you know will cause problems, such as words that would deceive your lies that you are telling.

Touching the cheek
By touching your cheek, you are showing signs of exaggeration or emphasis over something that is happening. Usually, both hands on both cheeks show exaggeration and surprise over something, or it could also be horror.

Reading the Forehead
The forehead will tell you vast amounts about what you can expect to understand about another person. While the forehead cannot really move much, it still can do many different things, such as wrinkles or sweat and this can be quite telling on its own. Most people tend to ignore it, but professional gamblers, who know that everything hinges upon them being able to bluff their way to their victories that they are looking for, will make it a point to hide their foreheads as much as possible to prevent others from knowing what they are thinking.

Wrinkled
When a forehead is wrinkled, this is usually due to a movement of the eyebrows. Typically, when you see someone with a wrinkled forehead, you can assume that they are emphasizing whatever they are making the eyebrows do or say. If you see that someone is furrowing their brows and their forehead wrinkles as well, it is like extreme disapproval or an extreme focus.

Sweaty
When you notice that the forehead is sweaty on someone else, there can be a few different reasons for it. They may find that they are exercising too much, and as a result, they are sweating. The temperatures in the area

may also genuinely be too hot as well. However, more likely than not, if the temperatures are not to blame, then it can apply either fear or arousal.

Touching the forehead
By touching one's forehead, you can read that they are trying to remove sweat. This is usually a signal that they are relieved about something, whether that something is a job finally completed or relief of a problem that they were going to have to face. When you touch your forehead, it could also be a sign of fear in which you are struggling to overcome. On the other hand, it could also be saluting someone to show respect or touching the head to imply thought.

Reading the Mouth and the Lips
When it comes to reading the mouth and lips, you can get a whole wealth of information relatively simply. All you have to do is pay attention to the way that the mouth and lips move, and you are able to start making out a lot of different types of emotions.

Flattening lips
When lips flatten together, you show that you are trying to hold your tongue—you want to avoid saying something. It could be that you disapprove but also would rather not offend the other person, or you may also feel like you need to speak but know that it is not the right place or time. Either way, it can be highly problematic if you see this. Assume that the other person does not have something nice to say.

Lowering lips down
When lips are pulled down, you usually are seeing some degree of sadness or displeasure that must be acknowledged. This is typically seen in a frown or a grimace of some sort and is indicative of that dislike of whatever else is going on.

Parting lips
Parting lips is highly important as well. When you see this, you know that the other person is flirting with you. This is even more the case when you can see that they are making gentle, coy eye contact with you or if you see their tongue coming out as well. However, this can also be indicative of simply wanting to talk to someone else while waiting for their attention.

Puckering lips
When you pucker lips, you show that you are not very certain about something that is happening. You have some reason to disagree with or dislike it.

Pursing lips
Pursing your lips is slightly different from puckering. While puckering is a kissing motion, pursing your lips involves pulling them in and closed.

It is usually indicative of some degree of tension, and you will need to turn to the rest of the body language as well to figure it out.

Raising lips up
When you see lips pulled up, there is usually a reason for it—and for the most part, it is positive. It is usually a smile, though it could also indicate feelings of disgust if you see other telltale signs of it.

Sucking on lips
When you suck your lips in, you pull them into your mouth to hide the pinkness of them. This is typically a sign of thinking and uncertainty though it can certainly also be a sign that you are trying to suppress something.

CHAPTER 6
Understanding The Movements Of The Body

At this point, it is time to start looking at the body and how you move it in general. We all hold our posture differently, and that posture that we have is always going to be indicative of the feelings that we have at the moment. Our posture is constantly shifting with our moods. You may be standing tall one moment, only to have the entire demeanor shift as soon as something frightening happens. When you see that someone else's body language is shifting a lot, you can use that to interpret what is happening around you.

Within this chapter, we have several key concepts to go over—we must identify open vs. closed body language first so we can then get through the rest of the chapter. Then, we will look at how some people move their bodies in open and closed manners. In particular, this chapter is focused on reading the arms, hands, and shoulders to begin creating that foundation to go along with the expressions that we looked at in the previous chapter.

Open Vs. Closed Body Language

Understanding the difference between open and closed body language is imperative. This is the most fundamental way to understand the behavior that you are exposed to just due to the fact that the language that you view will be predominantly either open or closed. Open body language signals that you are open to some sort of interaction with the other person—it conveys a receptiveness to being approached. Typically, open body language is positive, but it can be negative as well. In fact, aggression is often very open body language because it involves approaching another person. It will have a wider stance that you commonly see with open body language because of this. It is an openness to violence.

Closed body language, then, tells you that they do not want to engage with someone at all. It shows an attempt to close oneself off from the interaction entirely or to find a way to escape it. When you have closed body language, you are trying to retreat rather than approach the situation that you have at hand. This difference is imperative to understand—when you are closed off to others, you are trying to avoid that interaction entirely.

Usually speaking, open body language is relaxed and wider. It is more natural and at ease—it shows a calmness or a recognition that there is going to be an argument or a fight. It shows that there will be no escalation from the individual in particular. Conversely, closed body language is closed off—it often involves barriers or creating barriers with your body, such as using hair to obscure the face, a hat rim to cover the eyes, or even just arms in front of the chest to avoid being forced to interact further. It is uncomfortable and desperate for closure.

When you want to address the differences between open and closed body language, you want to look for signs of that receptiveness in general. You will be looking to see if eye contact is being made if they are trying to close themselves off, or if they are even positioning themselves in such a way that they would not be involved with you. Being able to see the differences in this is imperative: It requires you to understand just how likely an interaction is to go well or poorly. It requires an acknowledgment, a recognition that the other person has their own preferences and opinions and that those ought to be considered as well.

Reading Shoulders

We will begin at the top of the arms—the shoulders. When we read the shoulders, we are taking a look at what they are doing in relation to the body—are they held inward, outward, or neutral? Are they moving? Are they resting against something else? Pay attention to the ways that the shoulders are sitting if you want to start understanding whether someone's body language is open or closed. Generally speaking. However, you can assume that someone is closed off if they are tucking their arms inward toward themselves. If their shoulders are held tightly, it is probably due to closing of the body language.

Exaggerated shrugging

When you shrug with exaggeration, you are raising and rotating your shoulders around in a circle. You are preparing for some sort of battle, and it shows that you are aggressive in some way, shape, or form. When you do this, you are showing signs that you are potentially becoming threatening.

Leaning on a shoulder

When you lean on one shoulder, you pose yourself against a wall. This is showing a sign of comfort and relaxation. You are making yourself vulnerable because it will take precious time to push yourself out of that position, and that means that you would leave yourself open to being hurt if that was the desire of the other person. It is also a common sign of dominance or confidence because it shows that you have little concern that something is going to go wrong or that you should be worried about being in a vulnerable position. You think that you will be just fine, so you shift into this position in which you are not ready to fight back if necessary.

Relaxed shoulders

Keeping your shoulders relaxed shows that you are comfortable or relaxed. It shows that there is little tension that is holding you back and that you are not concerned about the current situation that you find yourself in. You may show that your arms are low and unimpeded as they swing about by gravity. This is the ultimate indicator of relaxation.

Shrugging

Generally speaking, shrugging is a sign of ambivalence or being unsure about a situation. It may be that you do not know how to answer, or you could just not care about it. Especially when you move with your palms upright and exposed, you show that you are being honest and not hiding anything as you navigate the situation.

Subtle shrugging

Subtle shrugging involves you raising and dropping your shoulders rapidly, but slightly at the same time. It could even just be a quick shift of your arms and nothing else. It shows that you are uncertain about a situation or that you are uncaring about it. It could also be a sign of lying about something.

Turning shoulders away

When your shoulders are turned away from someone else, you position yourself so your body is facing away, even if you are still looking at the person. It implies that you are done with the conversation or interaction. You are waiting for it to wrap up so you can walk away and be done with it entirely.

Reading Arms

When it comes to reading the arms, there are even more movements that can occur than when considering the shoulders. This is thanks to increased levels of dexterity. Generally speaking, the more dexterous a body part, the more likely that it is to have even more types of movements.

Crossing arms

Crossing arms creates an immediate barrier between yourself and the person across from you. This is one of the clearest signs of showing that you are entirely uninterested in interacting with the people around you. When you look at how to understand these crossed arms, you see someone that wants to create some sort of distance or shield between themselves and the other person. Consider this person closed off and work on opening them up little by little.

Expanding arms outward

When arms are expanded outward, you are doing one of a few things. It could be that you are showing that you are comfortable with the current situation. You want to display that comfort to other people, and you want to portray that you are willing to be open. Or, it could be that you are showing dominance or even aggression, depending on the other actions that happen as well. All things considered, however, it is a genuine form of open body language that must be interpreted as such.

Hiding arms

When you hide your arms, you try to cover them up somehow. It could be that you pull them away, or you shift them so they can be rested behind your back. It can show defensiveness if you pull away, or it could be confident if you are simply sitting there with your hands resting behind your back without a care in the world. Either way, you must look at the fact that you are showing that degree of confidence.

Pulling arms inward

When you pull your arms inward, you are shrinking away from an interaction. You are withdrawing yourself, trying to get away from it. This is textbook closed body language and shows a lack of willingness to proceed with the interaction. This should be taken quite seriously.

Raising arms above head

By raising your arms up in the air, you make yourself larger. You may be exaggerating your motion, or you could also be aggressive. Look at the rest of the body language that you are showing and then make it a point to put them together. You can usually assume that this is some sort of accentuation of whatever the rest of the body language is showing as well.

Reaching out

When you reach out toward someone else, the way to read it is entirely based on intent, along with the amount of force used. Generally speaking, intent to harm someone else is going to be very forceful reaching out, whereas if someone is much more gentle and careful as they reach out, they are usually making it a point to show comfort or kindness instead. Pay attention to the type of reaching out.

Self-hugging

Self-hugging is typically an attempt to self-soothe. Think about the look—you are reaching out and holding your side with one of your arms. You are showing that you are closed off and that you are attempting to calm down. You are trying to find a way to relax more so you can begin to engage more, or you are trying to hold it together long enough to get out of a situation that might not necessarily be as good as you want it to be.

Using arms as weapons

When you use your arms as weapons, you are making it clear that you are uninterested in being involved with those around you. You are making it clear that you are seeking space for yourself. You are lashing out at others. It could be in self-defense, or you could also be the instigator. This is entirely dependent upon the situation. However, it does show signs of aggression. The arms can be used as a club with a fist. It can slap. It can punch or jab. The hands are potent weapons that can be used strongly against other people.

Reading Hands

Finally, when you take a look at the hands-on people, you start to see so much more potential in their movements and actions. People generally try to hide their hands; however—hands are easy to read, and most people know this. However, if you learn to pay close attention, you can spot all the signs that there could be a problem that you must address.

Chopping hands through air

When you chop your hands through the air, you have your hand flat, and you slice it through the air. Sometimes, you will make it a point to hit the edge of your hand against the palm of your other hand. It is meant to show dominance. This is especially the case if you do so with your palms down. However, if you chop your hand with palms up, it can imply that you are trying to get people to agree to your credibility.

Clasping hands together

When you clasp your hands together, you are holding your own hands. This is typically indicative of restraint or an attempt to calm yourself down. It is supposed to show that you are trying to be steady. Usually, it is regarded as closed off behavior, especially if the hands are tense as they sit there.

Hands hidden

When hands are hidden, it is indicative of you trying to hide something. You are attempting to put your hands out of sight so they cannot be read—perhaps behind your back or in your pockets. This is quite closed off and shows potential for deception, or it could also be intense submissiveness as well.

Hands tightened in fists

When you tighten your hands into a fist, you show firmness when they are at your sides. It could even be deemed aggressive if you show other aggressive behavior as well. You will need to make the context clear to determine whether it is just stubbornness or if it is going to bridge over to overt aggression.

Hands on hips

Putting your hands onto your hips is usually showing openness. Though it is commonly misinterpreted as aggression or being forceful, it is actually a position of readiness for whatever is about to happen. It shows that you are willing to do whatever you have to in the future.

Height of the thumb

When you take a look at the thumbs, you can see that confidence is usually noted by having higher thumbs. Think about how you can grip your arms when you cross them. If your thumb is extended and put outward, it shows that you are pointing them upwards aggressively.

Holding onto something
When you hold onto something, you usually create some sort of shield or barrier for yourself. Think of the look of putting a phone or a cup of coffee between yourself and someone else. You might hold onto it in front of yourself, trying to make it, so there is something between you and the other person.

Pointing
Pointing is typically considered to be rude, but it is also an indicator of dominance and of aggression in some situations. It shows a sign that you are more in control of a situation or that you are asserting that you are above someone else. Think of how you may scold a young child with the use of a finger to point. It is meant to show sternness and scolding.

Showing hands visibly with palms pointing down
When you put hands out, showing them openly, but do so with the palms down, you are showing that you are in control of the situation. You are making it clear that you control what is happening and that you refuse to make any changes to what you are doing. You show that you are firm in the situation, but you also show that you are trying to be forthcoming about everything as well. This is often seen when you look at politicians or leaders trying to talk to a crowd.

Showing hands visibly with palms pointing up
When you show hands visibly with the palms pointing upward, you are showing signs of honesty. In particular, it is a plea for trust, showing that there is nothing that you are attempting to hide in that particular situation that you are in. You are showing that you wish to be deemed as being honest in the moment. This is commonly seen with pastors or priests during a sermon.

Steepling fingers
When you steeple your fingers together, your fingers are pressed against each other at the pads, though the palms and finger lengths never touch. It is very similar to the look of a roof steeple above someone. It is meant to show confidence and authority. It is a clear sign of dominance when you see this. It will usually be seen by leaders around a table, almost calculatingly.

The temperature of the hands
The temperature that your hands take on actually tells a lot about what is being felt in the moment. When your hands are colder, usually, the entire body is tense. This is because when you are stressed out, your body redirects blood to important areas such as your heart and lungs, while also filling the legs so you can run. However, when the hands are warmer, it usually shows signs of relaxing. This becomes even more relevant when you start looking at haptics.

Widened hands
When the hands are wide, you show comfort. This means that if you can see individual gaps between each of the fingers, or the hands are simply spaced out widely. This is usually noted by seeing the large width between fingers as they stretch out. When hands are narrower, it shows stress.

CHAPTER 7
Understanding The Movements Of The Legs And Feet

Next comes looking at the feet and legs to begin to understand people. Despite the truth, most people disregard the feet and legs as not mattering much for body language. After all, all they do is hold you in one place. They just keep you there, not doing anything at all. They don't move about. They simply stand there, supporting you.

But, the truth is that they are actually highly telling. Though there are not too many different positions that legs can go into—your ankle and knees only bend one direction. However, you can pose them in several different ways, from sitting crisscross to standing up or leaning from one foot to the next. You can do all of that with ease. These different poses can actually portray an awful lot about who you are, what you are doing, and why you are doing what you do.

However, reading the legs and feet requires a bit more nuance. It requires you to pay attention to more than just how the legs are posed. Men and women actually differ quite a bit in how they stand themselves around and what they do with their legs. This means that you must be willing to pay attention to this—you will need to make sure that you are looking at how someone is posing and then also considering their gender as well to get the clearest details as to what is going on with them.

Within this chapter, we are going to go over many different ways that people stand and sit. When it is specific to just one gender, it will be noted. When it is nonspecific, that, too, will be noted. We will look at both open and closed off body language from the waist down, both in sitting poses and in standing as well. This is the best way to ensure that you get a clear understanding of the body language with it all separated out nice and easily.

Reading Standing Legs in Open Positions

When it comes to reading legs in a standing position, you must take a look at what they are doing. Standing legs really do not have many options just by virtue of the fact that they do have to support your body. They can really only do that in so many different ways when you are standing up. However, there are still a few different ways that you can look at the movement of the body that will help you to figure out what to do or how to read the movements that you make or how other people move.

Neutral stance

The neutral stance is one in which people stand with their feet spaced evenly apart, usually right around shoulder-width. This is the pose that is used to convey relaxation and comfort. When it comes to looking at this pose, you can assume that the other person is perfectly content and comfortable with the situation.

Weight on one foot
When weight is just on one foot, it shows more relaxation. It is indicative that the individual that you are speaking to is content where they are—they are not interested in moving. They are perfectly content with their position and how they are doing. They want to continue the conversation.

Legs standing and crossed
When you see someone standing with their legs crossed, they are actually showing open body language. This is one of the only times where body language that folds in on itself is actually positive. When you stand this way, you are actually rooting yourself in place—there's no easy way that you can move from your current position, and that shows that you are driven to remain where you are in the moment. It shows that you want to maintain the interaction that you are having at the moment without trying to cut it short.

Planting legs widely apart
When you see that legs are planted widely apart, especially when that distance is wider than shoulder-width apart, you can assume that they are aggressive. These wider stances are meant to make the individual seem larger. They do not want to mess around any longer.

Long steps
When you see someone taking longer steps around somewhere, they are showing you that they are feeling confident and in control of a situation. You can see that they are comfortable in the position that they are in.

Reading Sitting Legs in Open Positions
Sitting down can be read in very specific ways as well. We can sit in all sorts of different forms that you can identify as being necessary. Some people will sit differently than others, and this is perhaps the most pronounced when you look at the differences between male and female sitting positions. Now, this may seem surprising, but consider the fact that men and women have different hips and pelvises—women are designed to have wider pelvic regions to allow for childbirth, and that is seen in their poses. Additionally, because women tend to dress differently, wearing skirts instead of pants, you can start to identify a lot just by paying attention to how people sit.

Men sitting widely
Men tend to sit wider than women—they will sit with their legs extended naturally. However, as confidence grows, so too does the distance spread between the knees. The more widely someone spreads their legs when sitting, the more confident they feel, and the more likely that they are to keep their legs widely spread.

Women sitting with crossed legs
When you see women sitting like this, it may be that they are closed off, but, if their legs are generally relaxed, and they look comfortable, there is likely nothing to worry about. They are probably perfectly content at the moment and will be just fine. When you look at them, they will have their legs together because they are taught to sit as such. This is to ensure that a dress is still modest enough to not flash other people.

Men using the 4 cross
Sitting in a 4 cross is sitting with one foot on the ground while the other foot is lifted up so the knee can bend with the foot on the opposite thigh. It creates a shape of a 4, which is where the name comes from. This pose is typically specific to men due to the fact that sitting this way would be revealing for women. When you see this, it is usually a sign of confidence. However, depending on how wide open it is, it could also be a form of cockiness as well.

Women stretching
Some women will sit with their legs stretched out. Typically, it is one leg stretched out over the knee or thigh of the other. Doing so makes the legs look longer, which women use to flirt. By stretching out the legs and making them look longer, women are able to show that they are interested in the other person. It is often a form of flirting and showing interest in the other person.

Feet planted on the ground
When the feet are planted firmly on the ground, it shows a neutral position in which you are trying to display that you are attentive. Women may also have just one foot planted on the ground with the other leg crossed to protect themselves from flashing other people.

Reading Standing Legs in Closed Positions
When you are closed off while standing up, your legs show this as well. Your legs will naturally be more resistant and may show that you do not want to be around the other person for any number of reasons. However, when standing, there are really only a few things that could show that.

Keeping feet close together
One thing that people do when they are closed off is to keep their feet close together. Doing this shows a degree of discomfort or even timidity. When you stand like this, you make sure that you have shrunk down—your feet closer together implies that you are standing closed off. It makes you smaller, so you are less of a target than if you stood widely.

Touching knees together
When the knees touch each other while standing, it shows nervousness. When this is done, it shows a position of shielding the genitals. This shows defensiveness, as well. It is more common in women than in men.

Taking smaller steps
When you stick to smaller, shorter steps, it usually shows that you are trying to avoid attention. You are trying to make sure that you are seen as less aggressive. It is sometimes seen as a sort of shuffle along to try to make oneself come across as less conspicuous.

Reading Sitting Legs in Closed Positions
Closed positions when sitting are quite apparent for men, while for women, they are a bit more nuanced. You must be able to look at what the woman is doing and pay attention to her body movements. When it comes to being able to tell what people are thinking when they are sitting down, for the most part, you will be paying attention to how they sit and how close their legs are together.

Women sitting with tightly crossed legs
Women with their legs tightly crossed shows that they are usually unwilling to discuss what is happening. It is a show of lack of interest in communicating further, especially in situations where you are talking to a woman, or when there are negotiations going on.

Men sitting with crossed legs
When you see men sitting with crossed legs, it is almost always a sign of closed-off behavior. They really only sit this way when they are uncomfortable or do not really want to engage in the current discussion. Remember, showing the crotch for men is usually a show of comfort and of being assertive in the situation.

Women sitting with ankles locked around each other
When you see someone sitting with their ankles locked around each other, they are usually used to holding each other in place. You have one foot hooking around the other. This is an even more extreme version of women sitting with their legs crossed—it is an extreme form of closing yourself off and then locking yourself away.

Legs hooked onto the chair
When you see that the legs are hooking around the legs of a chair, you see signs that someone is trying to close themselves off and anchor themselves. It is a sign of restraint most of the time, typically due to nervousness or discomfort. It is an attempt to convey unwillingness.

Hugging crossed legs
When you see someone holding their legs that are crossed, as if they are almost hugging them, you are usually looking at someone who is uncomfortable. It is a complete lack of willingness to open up at all, most often when you are stuck in close proximity to people that you do not want to be around.

Holding legs against each other
When you hold your legs so the knees touch, you are showing a sign of timidity, particularly in women. It is also a habitual position sometimes as well. This is very common in women who have been taught to sit this way due to trying to prevent yourself from revealing underneath a skirt or dress.

Reading the Feet
Finally, we get to the feet. The feet are integral in making sure that you are moving along, and they provide you with lots of support as well. However, they can also reveal plenty about your mind if you know what you are looking for. When it comes to looking at the feet, you can spot willingness to go, closed off behaviors, and more.

Watching direction of feet
When you pay attention to how someone moves their feet, you can actually get a clear image of their mindset. You can see that you will actually be able to tell what they are thinking about, what's in their mind, and what they really want if you pay attention to the direction that their feet are pointing. If you want to know what they want, you simply look down at the feet. They will always tell you what it is that the person has on the mind. People will have their feet point at other people that they are interested in engaging with, or in the direction that they want to walk as if their feet are preparing themselves to go out and claim whatever it was that they wanted in the first place.

Bouncing on feet
When you see someone bounce on their feet, you watch them primarily on their toes, rolling on and off their heels. This can do one of a few things—it could show you signs that they are nervous, or that they are anxious about something. It is an attempt to eliminate and alleviate that nervous energy in hopes of being free from it.

Pacing
Pacing is a clear sign of anxiety and nervousness, especially if the individual is pacing as they speak. Think about how sometimes, people pace nervously, wringing their hands as they try to talk to someone else because they are feeling nervous. This is another way to start eliminating that restless energy.

Playing with a shoe on feet
When women in particular allow their feet to slide in and out of their shoes, they are showing signs that they are attracted to someone else. It is a clear sign of flirting when a woman does this around someone else, and it works well to attract the attention of the other person as well. Typically, this happens with the woman sitting with her legs crossed so her foot can slide in and out of the shoe in clear sight of the other person.

Shaking feet
When you see someone shaking their feet, they are usually attempting to hide a lie. This is even truer when you can see that their feet are shaking underneath a table. This is most obvious when you realize that the table that they are sitting at is also shaking with the movement, or if you can see the movements of their clothing. It is a clear sign of anxiety.

Stomping the feet
When someone stomps their feet, it is meant to show a sign of firmness. Think of how children who do not want to change up what they are doing will stomp their feet in defiance. This can additionally show aggressiveness or anger, or it could show signs of a desire for attention as well.

Tapping feet
Tapping the feet is a clear sign of tension in a situation. It is meant to show that they are actually in a position of being tense. It could also be indicative of impatience as well. The more that someone taps along their feet, the more likely that they are to show that they are done or that they want the other person to realize that they are currently uninterested in the interaction.

Touching feet
When someone touches their feet, particularly with women, they show either suggestiveness or tension. Sometimes, a gentle stroke could be seen as flirty or suggestive while trying to squeeze. It shows a sign of a need for relief from the tension.

CHAPTER 8
Proxemics

Just because body language is typically indicative of actual body movements doesn't mean that there are no other important aspects to consider as well. In particular, being able to see proxemics is an incredibly important part of being able to understand what is going on with other people. The sooner that you learn to understand and acknowledge what it is that you must do to help other people understand your position, the better, and that means taking a look at the aspects of nonverbal communication such as how someone positions themselves relative to someone else as well. Think of, for example, how someone stands and how far away they may position themselves. This is an important factor to consider because you can see a lot about how someone feels or sees the people around them by looking at where they position themselves in space as well.

Think about it—you can move around a lot in space. You can be above someone or below them. You can be near to them or far from them. This is important to acknowledge—it will help you to understand precisely what it is that is happening between people. Learning to acknowledge proxemics will help you two ways—you will be able to firstly understand people. Additionally, you will also be able to utilize proxemics your own way to influence other people around you as well. There are so many different ways that you will be able to influence others when you start making use of them.

Defining Proxemics

Proxemics is quite simple to understand: It is the positioning of someone in space around someone else. You are taking a look at how they fit into the world around them and how they choose to allow themselves to be positioned so you can then begin to recognize how everything plays out. Because of how many options that people have when it comes to putting themselves somewhere in space, there are many other ways that you can look at the situations as well. Are they gravitating toward certain people? Are they putting certain amounts of space between themselves and those around them in hopes of being able to distance themselves? This is imperative to understand: When you see how they do choose to orient themselves in approximation to other people or things, you can start piecing together a lot about intent and feelings. Someone who shies away from someone else is probably interested in being kept at a distance while someone who is trying to be closer to them may find that they are much more likely to gravitate toward them. Learning to identify those feelings matters immensely.

Within proxemics, there are two key metrics that you need to pay attention to. You must look at how someone positions themselves vertically to get a good idea of what they are thinking about the other person. This involves figuring out how to position oneself either above or below someone else. You must also take a look at horizontal proxemics as well—how far away someone tries to get from someone else. These both work in different ways and should always be read separately for the best possible results.

Vertical Space

When you read vertical space, you are taking a look at how someone positions themselves compared to everyone else around them. Some people will intentionally make themselves look taller or shorter than other people for a reason. Other times, people will intentionally get down at eye level. The best way that you can encourage the interpretation of vertical space is to take a look at eye level as a sort of axis. Eye-level is oftentimes the default level, and from there, the higher or lower someone gets will show very different meanings as well. You want to be able to read this so you can understand what to expect.

Positioning yourself above eye level

When you start above eye level, you are trying to show that you are above someone else socially as well. You are trying to assert that your own personal social standing is higher, and therefore, you get that dominance or control over a situation. Think about how people who are trying to convey just how superior they are tend to try to position themselves so that they are looking down at someone else. This can even be accomplished through simply tilting the head back, so you give the illusion of looking down your nose at someone else.

You do not have to physically be taller than someone else to be able to be in this position. You can make sure that you are sitting in a higher position than everyone else, or you can choose to simply move your head just enough that you can still look down at someone else even if you are actually shorter than them. This is important to consider—it means that even if you see that you are in a position where you are smaller than the other people, you can still make it a point to be higher up than other people.

Of course, this is reserved for trying to look down on someone in the literal and metaphorical sense—you are making it clear that you are above them or that they are beneath you because you do not want to deal with them. This is usually rude, condescending, or even aggressive, depending on the context. It has a lot to do with intimidation attempts. It can be a boss trying to demand that someone else does something for them, positioning themselves higher up in a taller chair. It could be someone looking down their nose at you. No matter what, however, being above eye level typically comes with the connotations of trying to belittle or demean the other person.

Positioning yourself below eye level

When you position yourself below eye level, you do something different—you make yourself submissive or less threatening. It usually betrays a distinct lack of confidence in a situation and is a sign that someone is trying to make themselves smaller. It is usually seen with people who are shy, in trouble, or otherwise trying to make themselves less conspicuous. Below eye level is a sign that someone is trying to make it a point to make themselves smaller so they can stay out of sight. It also has a tendency to make someone feel inferior, as well.

Think of the effect that adults have on children when they are trying to scold them. Children usually feel frightened or intimidated by virtue of the fact that they are lower than the adult. This can happen to adults as well—they are intimidated by the appearance that they are less superior to others. This is an inherently unconfident, uncomfortable position, and that is precisely why people are told to keep their heads held highly when it comes to being able to boost confidence—sitting up with high heads actually helps with it.

Positioning yourself at eye level

When you position yourself at eye level, you are setting yourself up on even footing. By making sure that you are both on the same eye level, you will be able to make it clear to the other person that you value them as an equal. It shows respect and tact with the other person—it shows that you are not trying to dominate or threaten them and that they can expect you to be kind or understanding.

There are several different times where it is imperative that you put yourself at eye level if you are taller. This is precisely why, in business meetings, everyone's chairs adjust—it allows for everyone to be at eye level with each other. It is also why people are told to get down to the level of the children to talk to them as well. It is a highly important thing to remember—you can position yourself at the same level so you can show that openness to other people. This is the only level that is truly open on both sides of the interaction.

Horizontal Space

You must also consider the usage of the horizontal space around you as well. It is the distance that you want to put between yourself and other people. We naturally position ourselves closer to people that we trust or are close to emotionally, and we distance ourselves from strangers. This happens consistently, and when you cannot naturally position yourself as further away, you will make it a point to refuse to acknowledge the other person. This is why people can sit touching strangers on a bus or train without feeling distressed—they simply pretend that the other person is not there and ignore them to the best of their ability.

When you want to take a look at the distance that people hold themselves apart from others, you will see that there are primarily four different distances to look for. You can see people that position themselves closely together, choosing to do so within inches or feet while others choose to distance themselves significantly. Usually speaking, you will see that people will naturally fall into these patterns, and they are very predictable. This is why you can tell the difference between a couple that has clearly been together for a while and a couple of strangers. It's easy to spot that familiarity between people at a glance, and a major part of that is in looking at the horizontal space that they are maintaining between each other.

Positioning yourself in the intimate zone
The first of the positions that you can be in when considering the distances between people is the intimate zone. The intimate zone is the closest to positions. It is reserved for those that are the closest to you. It is those that are lovers, partners, or closest friends. Very few people are actually allowed to get this close to you. Generally, young children also get that option to be in the intimate zone for a period of time as well, usually until they start aging and deciding that they want their freedom. This is within just about one foot of the individual. It could also be touching as well, or anything in between.

When you are forced into this zone with someone that is not close enough to be within this space, you will typically distance yourself from them—you will engage in what is known as depersonalization. When you do this, you will intentionally make yourself stop thinking or feeling about the person as a person. You depersonalize them—you try to make it less comfortable for yourself by entirely ignoring the other person so that you can feel better about the situation.

Positioning yourself in the personal zone
When it comes to the personal zone, you are looking at friends and family members that are a bit more distant from you. It may be people that you know somewhat well, but would not be comfortable getting involved with on closer terms. When it comes to friends and family, you will generally allow some to get closer to others. Usually, the ones that are allowed to be closer to others are those that are closer friends. You may stand with a best friend much closer than to someone that you do not know very well. Your acquaintances will be kept further in the personal zone while your siblings or parents are probably much closer within this range.

The personal zone ranges between 1.5 and 5 feet of the other person. It is an important space to recognize. In this zone, you will sort of shift out who is closer and further to you. Most of the time, you will see that those closer together tend to like each other or be closer to each other than those that are further.

Positioning yourself in the social zone
When you position yourself in the social zone, you are putting yourself at a comfortable distance in which you would have no problems allowing other people to pass you by, even if you did not know them. Usually, you will allow yourself to be far enough away from people that you are unsure about. This is so you are not getting in their personal space, and they are not bothering you either. In this zone, you could ignore people without a problem, or you could choose to interact still without having to approach any closer.

Between 5 and 15 feet make up the social zone. This is the distance that allows for the most flexibility in terms of the interactions that you will have. When you keep people in this zone, you are able to avoid strangers or other people that you simply do not care to engage with.

Positioning yourself in the public zone
Finally, the public zone is a functional space at which you are far enough away that you can directly influence or interact with other people while a crowd of people can see you at the same time. This is the position where you try to keep yourself when you are trying to address several other people at any given point in time. By entering the public zone, you are interacting with people in a way that allows for you to be listened to. You position yourself roughly 12 feet away or further. Now that we have the creation of technology that will help with the projection of voice and image, the public zone can grow to be much larger as well. Think about it—you can be in the social zone even when you are thousands of feet away now in a stadium just due to the fact that your voice and image can still be projected for everyone else to see and hear.

CHAPTER 9
Haptics

The last form of nonverbal communication that we are going to address is that of haptics. Haptics makes up the ability that you have to communicate with other people via touch. It is a very important method to consider, especially due to the fact that touch can vary so much from person to person. Some touches are meant to convey happiness, comfort, or pleasantries. Other touches are meant to be hurtful. Others still are supposed to get attention from others, and there are still other types of hugs and touches that convey a desire to be closer or more intimate. All of this is important—it is good to be able to see the different ways that people touch each other. When you look at the different kinds of touches, you can start to identify the different kinds of relationships that people have with each other. Some people will touch in certain areas that have certain functional meanings. This is what haptics is—the communication made through touch.

Functional Touch

Functional touch is the first kind of touch to consider. These are impersonal forms of touching that are not meant to do anything one way or another. When you are looking at functional touches, you are considering the various different kinds of touches that are meant to be able to convey a purposeful meaning. They are the most commonly associated with different kinds of touches that are supposed to be used in professional kinds of settings. The more that you see this sort of touch play out, the more you realize that they are designed to simply convey respectful acknowledgment. Think of a handshake before negotiations—that is a form of functional touching. Additionally, a pat on the shoulder would be deemed functional as well.

This sort of functional touch is usually initiated by the dominant individual. It is okay for a dominant member of a party to initiate this kind of touching over someone that is less dominant. However, it is usually much less socially acceptable for someone else to instigate. It is not as acceptable for someone to touch their manager or boss as it would be for their manager to pat them on the shoulder.

Social Touch

Social touch is another important aspect that you must consider. When you look at the social touch, you are considering the different ways that you look at how people engage with those that they are close to. Usually, social touch is used by people attempting to touch those that they are engaging with on a more personal level. When you consider how people tend to engage with each other socially, you see non-vulnerable touching—touches that are limited. To certain areas that are not deemed intimate enough to be positioned anywhere else. When you see social touches, you see touches that are meant to be on the arm, hand, or shoulder. They are touches that do not immediately lead to you backing away from the other person. These sorts of touches are meant to be acceptable from even strangers.

Typically touches here are meant to redirect attention. For example, consider someone that is trying to get attention from someone else. For example, consider that someone just tapped on your shoulder to get your attention. This is a normal way for you to get someone else's attention that would not be considered too personal.

Friendship Touch

When you look at friendship touches, you are considering those that are designed to be friendly without actually instigating anything. Think of the way that you would touch a good friend of yours. You are not trying to be romantic or intimate with them—you are showing a platonic friendliness, and that friendliness should go far. When you are interacting with people who use platonic friendship touches, you will mostly notice that they happen between women. Men typically see these sorts of touches as an attempt to dominate instead of an attempt to get things right.

Friendship touches are reserved, then, for those that are actually somewhat close to each other. This can start to push past those points of closed-off areas, such as the waist or the lower back. When you are friendly with someone, you start to feel like you are okay, pushing past those boundaries a bit more often. This is essential—when you do this more, you are able to better build that closeness with people that will take you far.

Intimate Touch

When you look at intimate touch, you are pushing the touches past that friendship place. When you think of this, you can start to blur that line between romantic and friendship—they may happen in relationships that are not romantic, but, often, they are found within them. These are touches that are usually more likely to be seen as public displays of affection. You might see, for example, that you are hugging the other person, or that you are holding hands. This implies that the relationship is much closer than it otherwise would be. When you take a look at these sorts of relationships, you will be identifying general closeness between people.

Sexual Touch

Finally, when you consider the sexual touch of people, you will see that they are meant to be the most intimate. This is primarily reserved for lovers and partners and is designed as the most comfortable zone that you can be in. It is meant to establish love through intimacy. In general, you will see that though it is physically intimate, physical intercourse may not actually be the end goal. Sexual touches also include nuzzling up against a spouse, hugging them, kissing them, or touching them in a way that is primarily reserved for someone that you are going to be intimate with romantically.

CHAPTER 10
Identifying Body Language Clusters

Now, at this point, we have spent time looking over all sorts of situations in which you are able to understand how people are thinking. You have now seen several different ways that you need to read the other people in your life. From being able to see how people engage with each other and with you, you can start to figure out what it is that they want, what they like, and what they need. Being able to spot if someone is open or closed is perfect when it comes to trying to figure out just what it is that they are thinking or feeling. When you do this, you will be able to see just what it is that you need to understand. You will be able to see when you should be thinking about what the other person is trying to do. However, you need more than just understanding that certain movements usually mean one thing or another—you need to look at the clusters of body language as well. If you want to be able to understand what it is that is being conveyed properly; you must be able to also see the clusters of body language.

Remember, body language and nonverbal communication usually comes in clusters. It comes in groups that directly convey whatever it is that you are trying to say. Think about it: You could, for example, be lying to someone else only to realize that your body language is directly conveying that point. When you see that other people's body language comes into these clusters, then you can start looking for them.

Of course, those clusters of body language can vary greatly from cluster to cluster. For this reason, we are going to go through several common clusters of body language so you can start to understand what they all are. Some movements, as we have determined thus far, will have very specific meanings that you will have to keep in mind. When you consider these clusters, you should have an easier time starting to understand them.

Body Language of Dominance

Let's begin with the body language of dominance. This is a very particular type of body language that you can identify almost immediately if you know what you are looking for. Ultimately, the way that you can identify dominance is by making sure that you pay attention to posture, expressions, and also general demeanor. We'll go over three key points here: Creating dominant postures, creating dominant expressions, and fostering that sense of general dominance.

Most of the time, when you see someone in a dominant posture, you will see that they are wide open. You are looking at someone that is creating expansive, wide body language that is supposed to be confident. Dominance is often a form of confidence that is then made stronger or more assertive. It is making it clear that you are confident in your position and that your position is over someone else—you are asserting that you are in charge. There is a fine line between dominance and aggression that must be managed as well. You will need to pay close attention to this point and keep it in mind.

Dominant body language will require you to expand your body. You want to make yourself bigger than the other person—not necessarily literally, but spatially. When you do this, you are looking for ways that you can expand your body language, such as standing up taller, holding your head straighter, or even just trying to make yourself seem wider by standing with your arms and legs further apart.

As you walk about, you would expect to show signs of dominance as well—primarily, you would want to ensure that you are showing that you take wider steps. Remember, wideness is usually going to go hand in hand with confidence and dominance as well. If you want to make it clear that you are dominant, you will also need to make sure that you have the right expression as well.

Dominant expressions are usually those that are primarily neutral. The more unenthusiastic that you look, the better because that lack of enthusiasm appears disinterested and therefore, unimpressed. By having that unimpressed façade, you will see that you are actually in complete control over the situation. When you look at others with that disinterest, they will start to feel unnerved, granting the dominance that you were looking for.

Additionally, you will want to make sure that you make good use of eye contact as well. You want to make sure that you are maintaining proper eye contact at all times to ensure that you are actually showing the dominance that you need. If you want to make sure that you do your job and show that dominance off, you must make sure that you start with eye contact. Dominant individuals will make their eye contact long, even almost uncomfortably so, and they smile less as well. You will also see signs that the other person will avoid eye contact entirely sometimes as well—this is done intentionally to make it clear that the other person is not worth the time.

The most common body language that you can expect to see with dominant individuals, then, includes the following:

- **Hands positioned on the hips:** When you position your hands on your hips, you will find that you are positioned in such a way that you will be able to show your own assertiveness. Remember, hands on the hips are often positioned this way because they are meant to be at the ready—but it is commonly mistaken as an attempt to be dominant. Because of that, it is quite effective at showing that you are in control of a situation.
- **Showing off the crotch (for men):** Men, in particular, will utilize the quintessential crotch display when they are trying to make themselves dominant. Men will intentionally hold their

hands to their crotch to point out their crotches. This is done to try to say that their crotch is bigger, and therefore, they are more dominant.
- **Utilizing hair:** Some people, male and female, will intentionally use their hair to make themselves taller. They will intentionally style their hair so they have it higher up on their heads, therefore, making them a bit taller than they would be otherwise.
- **Utilizing touch:** Remember, in professional settings, you want to avoid touching people that are more dominant than you are. You want to make sure that you are putting yourself in a position where the more dominant individuals are able to be more above the others in context. This means that if you are the one that initiates the touching, you will be more in control of the situation and therefore, more dominant.
- **Walking in the middle of a path:** When you position yourself in the middle of a path, you force other people to have to move for you. You make it so that they will have no choice but to move over to let you through. This utter command of the space that you have makes it clear that you've got the position that you are in for a reason.
- **Wearing high heels (for women):** Some women will intentionally wear heels that will make themselves taller. Again, this allows for the creation of being taller. It is done to try to make the individual more capable of standing over others so that they can assert their dominance.

Body Language of Attraction

Now, let's take a moment to consider the body language of attraction. When you take a look at attraction, you can usually spot it almost immediately. Attracted body language is clear as day—it shows clear cut signs of being present just due to the fact that the individual is trying to make you see it. When someone is attracted to the other person, most of the time, they want the other person to take notice so they can determine whether it is reciprocated or not. When you want to take a look at this kind of body language, you will be looking for some unconscious signs that the other person's body is responding to you.

Of course, attraction has to be divided into male and female—the two sexes show vastly different signs that they are interested in someone else. Men usually are easier to read than women when it comes to identifying that attraction, and that means that you can usually tell at a glance how they are doing. If you want to ensure that you accurately identify what is going on with someone else, you will be taking a look at a few key signs. For men, these include:
- **Checking you out:** When he is attracted to you, he will check you out—and he won't be as discreet about it. He will be trying to

show you that he is interested and that he wants to make it a point to see more of you. This is important to him—he wants you to know that he considers you an option in case you may also consider him one as well.
- **Face touching:** Men who are attracted to someone else will also touch their faces more often. This could be in the ears, chin, cheeks, or anywhere else. It is part of nervousness, part grooming, and part sexual flirtation. People who are turned on by someone else tend to be more touchy with themselves due to their sensitive skin.
- **Flashing the eyebrows:** When you see that someone has flashed their eyebrows, they raise their eyes just slightly, and it is brief. It typically is a subtle sign, but it allows for more to be seen of the individual. This shows attraction is showing an attempt to widen the visual field because they like the other person. It also allows the other person to see more of their own eyes, which is key.
- **Grooming:** There are a multitude of different grooming behaviors that men who are attracted to someone else will show as well. IN particular, they may attempt to fix their hair or make sure that their clothes are just right. They want to look their best for those that they are attracted to. They may also make it a point to mess with buttons or fix their socks.
- **He touches you:** He will also make it a point to touch you while trying to explain it away as accidental. He doesn't want you to think that it is intentional, but he also wants you to know that he is interested, or trigger you to be interested in him as well. Additionally, he may plant his hand on your back as well, guiding you around and showing to others that he has already started to claim you.
- **Moving more often:** Men who are around someone that they are attracted to will naturally move around more. They will fiddle with things, run hands through their hair, or otherwise attempt to move around, hoping to pull the attention of the person that they are trying to attract to them.
- **Opening the face:** For men, when they are attracted to someone else, they open their faces. This is several different movements at the same time. They will show flared nostrils with raising their brows and parting their lips. This all works together to create an inviting look while also signaling that they are comfortable and interested in continuing to engage with that individual.
- **Parting the lips:** When men see someone that they are attracted to, usually, their lips will part briefly as soon as eye contact is

made. This is a clear sign of attraction, and you will be able to tell more if you can see the tongue moving slightly as well.
- **Raising brows when listening:** Men, when they are listening to someone that they are attracted to, will focus intently on what is being said. They will also make it a point to raise their eyebrows slightly, opening the face-up. This also serves to allow him to see more of you all in one go as well.
- **The crotch display:** Just as with dominance, you are likely to see the crotch display in attraction. When men point or emphasize their crotches, they want you to pay attention there so that they can get your attraction as well.

Women, when they are attracted to someone, tend to be a bit more subtle. They create simpler cues that are able to be picked up if you know what you are looking for. They include movements such as:
- **Eye contact:** Women make a very specific type of eye contact with someone when they are attracted to them. Usually, it is displayed by looking up at the person, then looking down at the lips before going right back to eye contact. The eye contact is usually through her lashes—she often tilts her head just right, so she has to look up at him.
- **Foot play:** Women will often play with their feet when they are attracted to someone, sitting cross-legged just long enough to be able to show off her legs to win you over.
- **Higher rates of blinking:** When some women blink regularly, they find themselves blinking far more often than they otherwise would have been. This is readily apparent if you pay attention. She will blink more often, and usually, her head will be tilted as well. She is batting her eyes at you in hopes of attracting you.
- **Playing with hair:** When she plays with her hair, whether twirling it around her fingers, tossing it over her shoulder, or otherwise, what she is doing is making it a point to show you that she is attracted. She shows off her neck and also pushes pheromones into the air.
- **She blushes:** You may notice that she finds herself blushing more often when you look at her—she can't help it! This is good—it is a sign that you're making her heart rate pick up and making her interested in you.
- **She displays her chest more:** Women tend to shift into a pose where they are standing with an arched back. By doing this, they push out their breasts and therefore, make them draw more attention. They may also push out their bottoms as well in hopes of making themselves more attractive to the individual. It is an attempt to display the body with hopes of the other person finding it attractive.

- **She gives you a seductive look:** The seductive look is what everyone constantly calls the bedroom eyes—it is looking at the other person with that look of longing and desire.
- **She laughs at everything you say, even if it is not funny:** Often, you will see that women who are attracted to someone think that they are the funniest person around. They can't stop laughing at them and will continue to find them entirely entertaining.
- **She leans in:** Women who lean into the other person are trying to get them to notice their attraction. She will make it a point to lean into you in hopes that she will be able to attract you and win you over.
- **She tries to attract you to her lips:** Often, women will make it a point to draw attention to their lips when they are attracted to someone. If she is on a date with you, she may make it a point to show you that her lips are there simply by wearing lipstick or trying to draw more attention to them by parting them.
- **The breathing rate:** She may not realize it, but her breathing will pick up in intensity and speed just slightly when she is around someone that she is attracted to. This is done because of the fact that attraction boosts the heart rate, which then increases the breathing rate. You can see this in particular if you were to take the time to look at her shoulders to pay attention to the breathing rate that she is showing you.

Body Language of Confidence

The body language of confidence is highly important—when you have the right, confident body language, you will find that everything else is so much easier to cope with. Ultimately, the way that you can get through having the right kind of body language is by making sure that you are able to interact with other people better. Having that proper confidence is essential if you want to be able to work well with others. If you are able to create a confident air to yourself, you would find that you can actually begin to be much more successful.

The truth is, being able to be confident is essential. If you cannot manage to maintain that essential confidence and that willingness to be out there and trust yourself, you are going to struggle. Confidence matters, especially if you are trying to interview for a job or otherwise need to make yourself assertive. Just being able to put yourself out there and show that you can and will be a confident person is often enough. However, that requires you to build up confidence in the first place.

The good news is, confident body language is often created simply through sheer confidence in general. If you want to make it clear that you are confident in the moment, you will want to make sure that you are paying better attention to everyone else. You want to ensure that you are able to create that degree of confidence that you will need, and you do that simply by starting to fake it. Yes—if you want to be confident, the best way to do so is simply through trying to pretend to be confident in the first place.

It all begins with having the right confident expression. To begin, you must make it a point to start with eye contact. The best way to be confident is to start with having the right degree of eye contact to ensure that you come across as comfortable. This is difficult to get just right, but confident individuals tend to use eye contact that follows the ratio of making eye contact 50% of the time during speaking and 70% of the time when listening to what someone else has to say. If you can follow this rule, you can usually ensure that you are on the right track. Additionally, you must make sure that you smile as well. Genuine smiles will help to show confidence, especially when paired up with the eye contact that you want to make.

If you want to get the right posture, then you will want to take a look at trying to create a welcoming position. This means that you want to balance being open and relaxed with confidence at the same time. This is because ideally, you should not be concerned about what other people are doing. You should not be afraid of what they will say or do, and you should be able to naturally allow your body language to expand outward. The more that you do this, the more likely that you are to find that you do feel more confident.

Most confident posture has a few key points to remember:

- **Stand up straight and tall:** Keeping your posture up tall will help you to be seen as confident more often. It will help you to be seen as someone that is in control of the situation. However, you want to be tall without looking down at the other person, which is reserved for being seen as dominant instead of just confident.
- **Stand comfortably:** You must also make sure that you are simply comfortable. If you are standing stiffly, it will become clear that you are standing in a way that will show that you are not confident or comfortable given the current situation that you are in. You must make sure that you pay attention to the positions that you use.
- **Keep hands visible:** Perhaps one of the easiest things that you can do to make yourself be seen as confident is to make sure that you stand up with your hands visible. Making sure that you keep your hands helps you to ensure that you are positioning yourself in a way that shows that you are not trying to hide them. In fact, you may even choose to talk with your hands, utilizing them to show that you do like what you are doing.
- **Show that you are listening:** When you make sure that you show that you are listening to the other person, you are seen as

confident. You are not concerning yourself with trying to pay attention to other aspects of what is going on.

Body Language of Insecurity

Insecurity is a type of body language that you will need to get to know. When you learn to read insecurity, you will start to see what it is that is on their minds. Usually, insecurity is visible when you consider the ways that someone engages with other people, and it is very important to understand it—when you know that someone is showing signs of insecurity, you can start to see that they have very clear problems. You will see that they are struggling and that you may need to offer comfort or help in some way to try to better the situation.

We all feel insecure at different points in time, and that is the most obvious when you take a look at body language. You might find that you are playing more with your hair or biting your nails. You may also attempt to play with items that will help you to displace energy. All of this is pretty typical, but you need to understand that they cause problems. They make you seem much less confident, and that can be a problem. If you appear nervous at a job interview, for example, you might come across as struggling to show your own degree of confidence. You make it clear that you are not actually trusting yourself, and that can be a major problem.

When you see someone showing that they are insecure, you will immediately be able to tell just due to the fact that their body language will be more closed off. They shrink inward instead of attempting to communicate outward. They will be unwilling to listen to other people due to their own stubbornness, or they may also cause problems because they pull away from others.

A common sign of insecurity is the creation of barriers between oneself and those around them. They want to make sure that the other people see that they are actively attempting to shield themselves. They want to ensure that their ability to shield themselves is actually heeded and that the other people will leave them alone. The most common creation of a barrier happens with arms. If arms are not crossed, then the hands may be shoved in the pockets instead.

Another telltale sign is to position oneself so that you are oriented away from the other person. You may find that you stick yourself in directions that show that you are not going to face the other person. You stand at an angle to try to prevent yourself from being directly faced as well. In seated positions, you might find your feet moving nervously. You may also see that they are hooked around the legs of the chair as well. It is possible that you will try to root yourself to your chair to be closed off.

When you are insecure, there are obvious signs in the face as well—you are likely to stand with little eye contact with the other person. You are too nervous to actually make it, so you try to avert your gaze as much as possible. Your brows are probably lowered as well in an attempt to shield your eyes because you do not want that direct eye contact with the other person. Additionally, you may chew on or lick your lips. This is not done in attraction here—it is because your lips are drying out due to your nervousness. The chin also tucks inward during nervousness and insecurity to make yourself smaller and less imposing to those around you.

CHAPTER 11
Using Body Language

Finally, we are at the end of the book. Now, it is time to be able to look at body language itself and how it tends to create influential behaviors for people. We are going to see just how you can begin to influence other people to create exactly what you are looking for. If you know what you are doing, you can actually heavily influence the way that other people interact. With the use of your own body language, you can begin to create all sorts of situations and expectations.

For example, consider that you want to influence someone so that they do what you want to do. If you know what you are doing, you will be able to change up how they tend to engage. Your confidence, for example, could influence someone else so that they will make it a point to change up what they are doing. Confidence sells. Or, if you want to get someone to stop doing something, you can assert that as well. There are also ways that you can position yourself to be deemed dominant over other people, something that is highly powerful as well. If you do this, you can start to recognize that you are capable of that influence.

Of course, if you know how to influence other people, you will need to be mindful of why you do so or how you decide to. When you want to influence other people, you must do so in a way that will help you—you want to make sure that you do so in such a way that is mindful of what other people are dealing with. You must ensure that you are actively making it a point to create that body language that you need in a situation, while also balancing out your expectations that you have for the other person as well. You should not just decide that you are going to force someone to do something to your own benefit.

Within this chapter, we are going to explore a few different concepts—we will be looking at the concept of neuro-linguistic programming, which heavily utilizes body language so that you can influence other people. From there, we will take the time to go over what you can do to begin changing your own body language. We will go over how you can change up what you are doing so that you are showing them what it is that you should be doing. Finally, we will explain several different uses for your own body language that will create the effects that you are looking for. As you learn to utilize this, you will get better at being able to control everything that you need.

Introducing the Concept of Neuro-Linguistic Programming

Neuro-linguistic programming, also commonly known as NLP, is designed to create the effect of influencing the behaviors of someone else just by making use of the way that you move or speak yourself. NLP takes control of your nonverbal communication that you use and then utilizes your own movements to influence the unconscious mind of the other person.

Think about it—when you utilize NLP, you are going to be changing up your body language so that you can get the other person to do what you want. You can change up your body language to influence them to say yes to something, for example, or you can mirror them to make them like you more to allow yourself to better influence them as well. NLP works as a way that you can essentially control the other person without having to do a thing. Through being able to make these differences in your own behaviors, you will see that you can actually control other people, and that is highly powerful and compelling as well. If you keep it up, you can begin to make more use of it. You can ensure that you are on the right track when it comes to influencing other people.

NLP was designed originally to grant average people who know little about psychology the training that they would need to control themselves. When you utilize NLP, you are able to begin controlling yourself and those around you. Consider this—you are trying to become more confident. However, the more that you try, the less that you do because you are stuck. You find yourself completely caught up with the negativity that you feel, and you never actually improve your behaviors. As this happens more and more often, you will begin to see that your own negative thoughts get worse. However, with NLP, you can start to influence them. You can start to change up those thoughts to grant yourself that ability to better change your mindset as well to create positivity instead. This can be done through all sorts of different possible options. If you're interested, you may want to check out a book dedicated to NLP—there are many of them, and you can find that there is a lot more to it other than simply utilizing unconscious behaviors to control thoughts and feelings.

Changing Your Own Body Language

If you want to be able to influence the behaviors of other people, the best starting point is in making sure that you look at how to identify your body language when looking at how it plays out in regards to others as well. If you want to be able to have that confident body language, you must first learn those steps to ensure that you change up the body language in the first place. Thankfully, changing your own body language is not as hard as you probably think—you can actually do so relatively easily.

With just a few steps, you can start to change up your own body language. With just a few simple changes toward how you approach your situation and what you do, you will be able to see that you have far more power than you gave yourself credit for. It won't take you much—you just have to try. It will get easier over time—you will become fully capable of figuring out what you need to do and how to do it. You will be able to do it at will after enough time, and that will be powerful.

Step 1: Start with identifying your body language as it is
First, you will begin by checking on your current body language. What are you doing in the moment? How are you feeling as you sit there? What is it that your body language is currently conveying? Is it positive or negative? Is it related to what you want it to be? Would you rather find a way that you can communicate something different? The beginning point is making sure that you know what you are doing so you can then make the changes over time. Start out with this idea of what you are doing in the moment so you can move on to the next step.

Step 2: Think about what you want to convey
From there, it is time to figure out what it is that you are trying to convey to the other party. Figure out what it is that you want to convey to the other person. Do you want to be happy? Frustrated? Annoyed? Figure that out and make note of it. That is the next big thing: You must make sure that you change up your body language to ensure that you are on track. When you know what it is that you want to convey, you can then move on to the next level.

Step 3: Begin altering the expression
Step 3 helps you to begin making it clear what you are trying to convey. You will begin to assume the expression of what it is that you are trying to get across to the other person. If you are trying to be confident with them, then you would attempt to assume that expression. If you are trying to be dominant, you would take on a dominant expression, and if you wanted to attract someone, you would show them that as well.

Step 4: Alter the posture
Once you've got the expression down, you start changing up your pose as well. You would begin to take on the right posture to show that you are, in fact, confident in the behaviors that you are attempting to create. The posture will help you to begin to alter the way that other people see you.

Step 5: Practice
Finally, you must make sure that you get better. Being able to change up your behaviors so that you can then influence other people takes serious practice—it is not exactly easy to just wake up one day and decide that you are going to start changing up how you behave. You will have to take the time to get to know the people around you. You must learn through experience that it is something that you can do in the first place.

Using Body Language
When it comes to mastering the use of body language, you must make it a point to utilize the different types of emotions that you want to convey. It does take practice, but, over time, you will find that it is actually somewhat easy to do when you can master it. We are going to go over several different ways that you can begin to utilize body language to

create the different effects that you are looking for. The sooner that you learn these, the sooner you realize that you can do better.

Mirroring

Before you begin any sort of influential movements to other people, you must make sure that you have the rapport to do so. You must ensure that you are on the right page to ensure that you are on track to ensuring that they are better capable of following along with you. You will need to ensure that you choose out behaviors that you know will be helpful for you. If you want to make sure that you are able to influence others, then you start out learning to mirror. As you develop rapport, you get better at also influencing other people. Thankfully, this is a simple process—you just have to know where to start.

To begin, all you have to do is start feeling like you do have a connection with the other person. When you do this, you begin to build up that relationship between you both. Take some time feeling like you are genuinely connected to the other person. Then, when you feel that connection, it is time to start using it.

You don't want to start out with simply changing your body language to match theirs—this can be too apparent if you are not very familiar with the other person. But, what you can do is match another aspect of their body language. You can choose to match their vocal cues instead. By doing so, you create the same effect, but it is harder to catch on that you are being copied if you are only being copied in mannerisms of speech. In particular, you will want to make sure that you match volume, speed, and fervor of speaking.

Then, with that match, you need to identify the punctuator that the other person is using. This is what they use to create a major sort of influence on what they are doing. You will want to watch how they talk. When they say something that they want to emphasize, they will do something. There will be some sort of mark. They might, for example, make it a point to raise their eyebrows, or they might move their hands a certain way. When you figure out what it is that they do, you can then utilize it. In order to mirror them, then you must make use of their punctuator so you can convince them that you do understand them. The next time that you sense that they would use their punctuator, you make it a point to do so instead. They then get the sense that you know them far better and that you understand them. This allows the creation of rapport.

To determine if you have succeeded, all you have to do is make it a point to move and see if they copy you. Do they move along with you? If they do, then they have picked up on your change in behavior, and they've chosen to adopt it as well. This is perfect for you—it means that they will be more receptive to everything that you do.

Nodding for influence

One way that you can begin to influence other people is simply by making it a point to nod your head when you ask a question. Did you know that through simply nodding your head, you can influence the other person to start to feel compelled to say yes to you? This is commonly used by people trying to practice NLP, and it can be used easily.

To begin, you will want to make sure that you are on good terms with the other person. This is commonly done through mirroring, but if you have a good relationship already, you can make use of this easily. For example, imagine that you want to ask your partner or spouse to do something. You would get their attention, and you'd want to make sure that they were looking at you. Then, as you make eye contact, you can start to nod your head to them. You can start making it clear that you are interested in asking them something. Then, you will want to nod your head, but the catch here is that you cannot be conspicuous about it. They cannot know what you are doing, or you will find yourself making it less likely that you would be able to get them to agree to what you are asking.

As you nod your head, you should do so barely perceptibly. This will influence them to start nodding their head slightly as well. This is because we naturally mirror those that we are close to. If you are close to your partner, you will find that they will copy you naturally, and you will then be able to make use of their natural inclination to follow your pace.

When they start nodding their head as you ask the question, you put them into the right mindset to say yes to you. You put them into that mindset that you can utilize to ensure that you do get what you want.

Positioning yourself as dominant

Another trick that you can use your body language for is to make yourself seem more dominant to the other person. When you are able to position yourself just right, you can actually win negotiations much easier just by virtue of the fact that you will be able to shift your behaviors. For example, many CEOs will position themselves just the right way to ensure that they are dominant in just about any situation. They will make it so that their chair is higher and then place a chair that does not have adjustable settings across from them. In doing so, they create a situation in which the other person is naturally underneath them. This allows their dominance to be asserted naturally, even if they were shorter and without having to do anything much at all to make it happen. Just by virtue of positioning them at a different level, you will see a big change.

Dominant body language can also be used to expand out around other people—you can choose to make yourself wider, more likely to extend yourself, or otherwise just by virtue of pushing yourself out wider. Take up more space at a meeting at the table, and you will naturally be seen as more dominant. Make people wait for you or otherwise utilize wider steps to show that you are bigger than the other person. This will naturally allow you to begin changing up the mindset that the other person has without them even realizing it. Just by virtue of being able to do this, you should be able to see that they will change up how they approach the situation as well.

Setting the pace
You can also utilize what is known as setting the pace to allow yourself to be more capable of influencing a mindset that the other person may have as well. One such way to do this is to first match the pace of the other person. This could be a literal pace in walking—you would simply step along with the other person. You'd make sure that you were lined up just right to start matching them from the beginning. Or, if they are tapping on the table, you could match their tapping. Essentially, you begin by mirroring the other person first. You want to make sure that you are following along with their behaviors before you then try to change them. In matching their pace, you do something very important with your own body language. You tell their unconscious mind that you are on good terms with them. You are showing what is known as rapport—essentially meaning that your relationship is good.

Then, as you continue to match their pace, you can start to alter it. You can start slowing down in a literal sense if you are walking alongside them. By making sure that you are walking at the same pace, you can make sure that you are both moving the same way. The hope is, as you do this, you will watch them continue to match pace with you. They will naturally change up their own body language to ensure that they are on the same page. They will naturally take the same pace as you just by virtue of the fact that they believe that the rapport is already there.

By doing this, you get control over some basic actions that can actually have massive changes to the body language of the other person. You can get them to relax or stop doing something nervously if you know what you are doing. You can get people to match your speed, or you can convince them that they need to change up what they are doing in other situations as well. The more that you work on how to do this, the better off you will be. This is a very important skill to develop if you want to make sure that you get those good influences.

CONCLUSION

And with that, you've arrived at the end of the book! You now know everything that you would need for a cursory understanding of what you need to do if you want to analyze other people. Being able to analyze others is highly powerful. It is influential, and it will help you to navigate the world better—the more that you learn to read other people and understand them, the easier it becomes for you to get through everything. As you become more skilled at being able to make those choices that you need, you will discover that you can actually do far better. You can start to come up with all the ways that you can better engage with people. You will be able to begin working better with people all around you.

The ability to read other people is powerful. It will help you to become more confident in yourself, and it can also help you to influence other people. You can use it to avoid being lied to or get along with people better. No matter the purpose, however, you now have the skills that you would need to ensure that you are on the right track. You now have the skills that you would need if you wanted to ensure that you could do more.

Remember, with this kind of power, you can begin to influence other people with ease. You can begin to change up what they do, how they do it, and why. However, with that skill, you must also acknowledge that you need to do so in a positive manner. You must acknowledge that you need to do better so that you can properly engage well with those around you. By learning to master this fact, accepting that you need to be responsible for what you do with this power, you will realize that you have far more options than you thought possible.

And now, as this book comes to a close, it is time for you to start considering what you will do, how you will do it, and why. It is time for you to start figuring out what you want to do. It is time to begin putting the information that you have learned here to good use. How do you choose to use it? Will you allow yourself to become more confident? Will you allow yourself to step back? Will you step forward? What will you do to ensure that you are on track with what you want, your goals, and how you want to live life? This book provided you with the tools that you would need, but now it is up to you to master them. It is up to you to figure out what you will need to do if you want to be able to become someone that is more confident, more aware of what you are doing, and more able to be certain that you are ready to succeed.

Thank you for taking the time to read through this book. Hopefully, as you did read through this book, you found that it was filled up with all sorts of important information that you can use for yourself. Hopefully, you feel much more confident in your ability to navigate social situations, and hopefully, you feel ready to take on the world. At this point, what you do next is entirely up to you! You can take it all on, or you can choose to allow the knowledge to go unused. No matter what, however, if you found that this book has helped you in your goals, please consider heading to Amazon to leave a review! Your feedback is always greatly appreciated!

DESCRIPTION

Are you sick of trying to understand other people, only to feel like you are completely and utterly lost? Are you done with constantly misunderstanding what people are trying to convey to you because you can't seem to understand the most basic of body language when you try to? If so, then keep reading... this book is for you.

Being able to understand the body language of other people is highly important—being able to see what it is that people want or need in a situation is great—it helps you to figure out what it is that you will need. It helps you to understand that ultimately, they are trying to communicate something to you. Especially because of the fact that your unconscious mind controls your body language and your actions in general, you want to be able to see what it is that drives people to do what they do. Through watching body language, you can tell the difference between people who are wide open with each other and people who are not. You can see the difference between being willing to engage with someone and being afraid of the people around you.

These skills are highly beneficial to you. They can help you when it comes to being able to negotiate. They can teach you how you will be able to better get what you want. You will be able to interview better, to avoid being lied to, and to attract more people simply because you will know that you understand their thoughts. You will be able to see what it is that you are doing. You will be able to see that ultimately, through recognizing your abilities to read people, you can succeed.

In this book, you will learn exactly that—you will learn the ins and outs of reading people's body language. You will learn how to tell what it is that those around you need. Little by little, you will learn about reading expressions, about how to see body language and understand other types as well. You will learn to read haptics and proxemics. You will also learn about how to use your own body language to influence other people as well. These skills matter, and the sooner that you recognize them, the better.

In particular, you will find:
- Why reading people matters and just how important it can be
- What you will need to do to read other people
- How you can begin to recognize the differences between different kinds of body language
- A guide to reading nonverbal communication
- Recognizing how to read expressions
- Learning to read the different movements of the human body, sitting, standing, open, and shut
- Recognizing how to change your own body language to utilize it
- The most common body language clusters and why they matter
- *AND MORE*

Don't let another day pass by—scroll up and click on BUY NOW today! IN doing so, you will discover that being able to read other people is easier than you thought, and you will be able to master these skills.

www.ingramcontent.com/pod-product-compliance
Lightning Source LLC
Chambersburg PA
CBHW071407070526
44578CB00002B/503